WITHDRAWN

CAPTAIN DAD

THE MANLY ART OF STAY-AT-HOME PARENTING

PAT BYRNES

Guilford, Connecticut
An imprint of Globe Pequot Press

I dedicate this book, as I do my life, to my lovely and loving wife and our precious children.

Lyons Press is an imprint of Globe Pequot Press.

Fourteen of the cartoons in this book originally appeared in the *New Yorker*. The illustrations in this book were created in pencil, pen, watercolor, crayon, colored pencil, digital, and whatever else was handy at the time, on whatever medium was also available.

Project Editor: David Legere
Layout Artist: Joanna Beyer

Library of Congress Cataloging-in-Publication Data is available on file.

ISBN 978-0-7627-8520-9

Printed in the United States of America

10 9 8 7 6 5 4 3 2 1

Contents

Introduction

I was a cartoonist. I made my own hours. My wife had a more traditional job without the flexibility. From a purely practical standpoint, it made sense that I be the one to stay home with the kids: I was home already. I gave it no more thought than I have just given it. Which is still more than I had given it in my life up to then.

Then the baby came. And there was no time to think about anything. There was only doing. Then my wife went back to work. And I was the only one doing it. The Primary Care Giver.

Got that? Primary. This is my full-time job. 'Round the clock. 'Round the calendar. So if you see me on the street with my kids (as if you would see me any other way), don't ask me, "Giving mom the day off?" I'm not filling in for my wife. I'm nobody's substitute. I'm the guy in charge, and I'm doing this my way. The guy way. Don't call me Mr. Mom.

Say hello to Captain Dad!

CHAPTER 1

The Words All Women Have Been Waiting to Hear

I became a parent at the tender age of forty-five. And I wasn't simply living in my parents' basement up until that time. I had had a career. Several, in fact. I had been an aerospace engineer, an advertising copywriter, a voice actor, and a cartoonist. And I overlaid those with countless moonlighting quasi-careers in multiple disciplines. I had directed radio commercials, produced live shows, and been a nuisance in statewide political campaigns. On the side I even renovated an old, beat-up house with my own hands, swinging a hammer from the hour I woke to the minute I collapsed, for months on end.

Bottom line: Hard work didn't intimidate me. Twelve-hour days, six days a week was not a deal breaker. Crushing deadlines, ultracompetitive backbiting, and unpredictable last-minute changes were par for the course. It was a life on the brink, but I was an unrepentant workaholic, and stress was a comfortable old friend.

So. Becoming a stay-at-home dad? Why, that should be a walk in the park, and I didn't mean just literally. Raising a kid? Child's play! Of course, this was before I knew what that phrase really meant.

Today, having been at it around the clock and calendar for more than eight years, I have to concur with what women have been saying for centuries.

I'D RATHER
BE WORKING

Being a stay-at-home parent is the toughest job there is. For a woman *or* a man.

There. It's been said. By a man. So it has to be true. Cut out this page, ladies. Frame it. Buy copies for your mothers and grandmothers. You have been vindicated. Men were wrong for pooh-poohing and nodding their patronizing assent simply to end the conversation. Wrong, wrong, wrong. Dead wrong.

But now a man has admitted it. In print. I'll even say it again in my deepest, manliest baritone, on behalf of every human male, using those three little words every spouse longs to hear.

You were right.

I am sorry you had to wait so long for that. The trouble is, there just aren't that many of us who understand how hard this job truly is.

But that doesn't mean that men don't *suspect* how hard it is.

Scientific surveys have found that nearly one out of two married men says he would love to do this. And I don't mean that the scientific surveyors asked two guys and one of them nearly said yes. I mean nearly 50 percent of the literally *several* guys who got cornered by this question said yes. I think their verbatim answer was, "Yes, dear."

So, how many guys actually follow through on that? According to the 2010 census, only around 158,000 American men stay home full-time to watch the kids for at least one year. Or one in 163 dads.

One in 2 says he'd do it; but only 1 in 163 actually does it. What does that tell you?

Exactly! It tells you that, in any sex-related situation, men *lie*.

Take me, for example. I said, "I work at home, I make my own hours." What I really meant was, "I had been searching for twenty-five years before I met you. I'll do *anything* not to face another twenty-five years of rejection!"

Instead, now I face twenty-five years of giving my two daughters my every ounce of sweat, attention, love, determination, patience, worry, guidance, trust, insight, worry, hope, passion, worry, and worry. All so they can grow up, finish school, and leave me for lives of their own.

Surely, letting them go will be the hardest part. But I figure that what I am doing now—The Hardest Job in the World—is preparation for that. It should leave me too exhausted to hold onto them for a minute longer.

CHAPTER 2

Now What?

You just got home from the hospital with the baby. You're awash in excitement and cute little blankets and pithy insights like, "Your life is going to change completely." But while you're tired from trying to sleep on that ridiculous foldout in your wife's hospital room, you're not yet bone tired from three consecutive weeks of the sleepless nights to come. And let's not forget the excitement of seeing the meconium give way to poop you can actually wipe off your baby's butt with something less toxic than kerosene. Most of all, however, you have your wife with you. Your wife whom you once loved a whole heck of a lot, but now love in mind-boggling new ways as she nestles your newborn against her breast. You don't even feel jealous about the boob competition. Talk about love!

But.

Now what? What happens next?

Life. Life is what happens next. It is messy and unpredictable, but that's the last thing you want or need to hear right now. You need something concrete to hang onto. So here is some concrete guidance on the concrete stuff you do and do not need.

New Baby Things You Can Live Without

- *A million baby how-to books.* Find one that answers the most pressing questions you have at the moment and stick

with that one. If there is a "best" answer, then you'll find the same answer in all the other books. If not, you'll find different answers everywhere, and you won't be in a mental condition to comprehend that all that means is that there *is* no best answer. And this will only make you start to worry. So why not be happily deluded that you have the best answer right there in your favorite new baby manual—as long as it is not this book. I can't handle that responsibility.

- *So damned many receiving blankets.* Theoretically they can be used for swaddling the newborn. Except, in practice, they can't. They aren't long enough. The only blanket that really works well for that is the one the baby is wrapped in when she comes home from the store. I mean hospital. And you can't put a nonswaddling blanket in the crib for months and months. So the rest of the blankets will simply end up cluttering your house, waiting to be repurposed as imaginary boats and forts and other obstructions to the walkways of your home.

- *Silver spoons.* What could possibly be a better way to welcome a baby to the world than with a silver spoon or baby rattle from Tiffany's? I mean, at least for someone who has no clue that to be "born with a silver spoon" is never said *nicely* about anyone.

- *Anything dry-clean only.* I mean, honestly! Who would ever think to give dry-clean-only anything for the baby or anyone who may come in contact with the baby? What's next, silk burp rags?

- *Anything white.* See above.

- *Socks.* Unless you actually enjoy having more to pick up around the house. Or unless you intend to hold them on with duct tape, in which case perhaps this whole parenting thing isn't the thing for you.

New Baby Things You *Can't* Live Without

- *Diapers.* Seriously, if you want to be the big winner of the unofficial Best Baby Shower Gift Competition, buy somebody a case or two of diapers. The mother-to-be will look at you like you are crazy—until the baby comes. Then you will be her hero for life. Meanwhile, all the other moms and dads at the shower will be kicking themselves for not thinking of it first.

- *A diaper bin that honestly, truly seals in the smell.* That should be obvious, but do shop around with this in mind. Also, you may want to keep a stash of plastic bags—bread bags, shopping bags, those roll-and-rip bags from the produce section—near those play areas that are far from the diaper bin. They can serve as temporary diaper storage and shave

miles off your pedometer. Ordinarily I'd say that all that extra exercise is good for you, but in the first year of a new baby, you need to conserve every electronvolt of energy you can.

- *Burp rags.* Remember the old-fashioned cloth diapers? These days they are used mainly to throw over your shoulder when you're holding the baby. Because babies spit up. A lot. For no apparent reason except that today was the day you ignored my previous advice and chose to wear a dry-clean-only sweater.

- *Big red ball.* Or blue or purple or whatever color. You don't need to go out and get one; you already have one. It's that thing you bought to sit on to improve your posture or to lean backward over to do sit-ups—but ended up stuffing in a closet instead. Well, now is the time to free up some storage space and pull it out again, because your newborn will have a "witching hour" each day, where nothing calms her except being bounced. It is an "hour" that can last several. I don't care if you already have thighs of spring steel and can do a million squats, sleep deprivation will rob you of your normal prowess, and you will be worn-out in a hurry if you don't have a big ball to sit on and bounce until your baby is reliably asleep. And then maybe you can steal a few winks yourself.

- *Advil.*

- *Tummy time mat.* When we were kids, our parents laid us on our tummies all the time. That's why we all died in infancy. But we did develop strong neck muscles. Today kids have floppy necks because they spend all day and night safely on their backs and never get a chance to learn to hold their heads up. Except during tummy time. That's when you lay your baby on his belly for ten minutes to listen to him scream at the outrage of it all—"Don't you know this could kill me!" (Okay, he says it in baby talk, but you get the message loud and clear. Especially loud.) It helps if you have a mat to lay him on that is not only comfortable, colorful, and entertaining, but also protects your rug from the inevitable spit-up. Or you could just use one of those million blankets you have.

- *Car seat carrier.* You already have to prove you have a car seat before they will even let you take your baby out of the hospital. But you will quickly find that the car seat is a handy all-around carrying case for your baby. A car seat carrier is basically a stroller base with wheels. You simply set the infant car seat on top of it, snap it in, and—*voila*—you have an instant stroller without having to transfer the wriggly bundle from one set of straps to another.

- *Camera.* I hate to be so retro but, really, you want something better than your phone for those early moments.

- *Snappy T-shirts and feety pajamas.* These are all your child will live in for her first few months. The T-shirts snap open and closed, so you don't have to pull them over the baby's soft, floppy head. And the jammies have snaps on the inseam for easy diaper changes. Absolutely essential.

- *Sleep sack.* This is a sleeping bag with shoulder straps. At first, babies can't have a blanket in the crib because of smothering hazards, and later their wriggly bodies can't keep one on for more than two minutes. I wish they made them for kids older than two.

- *Ball and chain.* Er, I mean baby monitor.

- *Pocket knife.* Just a little baby-size Swiss Army knife will do. At first you will use the blade to open boxes and cut other packaging and the teeny scissors to cut tags off of everything and snip through the million bands and bindings that stabilize toys in their packaging to prevent the toys from shifting during shipping or a near-nuclear blast. Later, however, you will find it useful for things like slicing and peeling apples (which you could do with the edge of a credit card, but it's a little messier) and snipping straws so they don't poke your kids in the eye when they're learning to drink. And a gazillion other uses. Why more moms don't carry pocket knives is utterly beyond me.

Now that you have all of your equipment, you are ready to begin parenting. The first thing you should do, if you are indeed just beginning, is to put this book down and SLEEP! Seriously, don't miss an opportunity to steal a few alpha waves. Not much skilled parenting is necessary in those first few months anyway, which is fortunate, because new parents typically don't have much skill yet. Face it, if it took an expert, the species would have died out eons ago.

In the beginning, parenting is mostly feeding, wiping, and trying to figure out the baby's rhythms. And trying to teach the baby to sleep. Parents try all kinds of things, like driving around the neighborhood for hours because the baby only sleeps in the car. We simply let ours sleep in the car seat—which itself was nestled in an heirloom cradle.

Others walk the baby in a stroller for hours. One of my girls would only nap in a sling, bundled up against me like a pea in a pod, sucking on my finger for a pacifier. I could have gone on a crime spree back then, as long as I only touched things with the finger whose prints had been sucked smooth. When she got older, she'd only nap in the battery-powered swing.

Captain Dad Tot Tip:
Save on shredding! Just throw all your old tax returns, credit card bills, and other personal papers away in the diaper bin. Then, if somebody does steal your identity, you'll feel like they earned it.

Whatever works. That's what you need to find and focus on. Especially once your wife's maternity leave is over and your solo career begins.

Right now your baby's sole job in life is to grow. And bond. Okay, two jobs. Yours is to facilitate those. Keep it in your head as that simple, and you'll do alright. Sure, it becomes technically more difficult if you have more than one child, but the principle holds.

So I really don't want to make this Getting Started thing seem more complicated than it is. Perhaps it would help to give it some historical perspective.

Some Historical Perspective

Throughout history, and prehistory for that matter, the top priority of a parent has been, very simply, to keep the children alive. This has meant, variously over time, protecting her from fanged predators, armed marauders, and trans fats.

But there are *some* days—like when the baby woke you at 4:00 a.m. because she couldn't breathe through her stuffy-head-cold

—NOW—

boogers, and your older daughter, who didn't want to go to sleep last night ("Ever!" she declared), didn't pass out until after 10:00 p.m., then leapt out of bed at the first excuse, such as that 4:00 a.m. incident with the baby screaming, and you're on your own because your wife is away on business, and you've almost made it to lunch, but your overtired elder child is melting down while defiantly maintaining that lack of sleep has nothing to do with it, and the baby is squirming out of your arms as you are trying to carry her over a safety gate, but you're too tired to lift your leg high enough, and it doesn't help that your jeans are binding because they are riding low because you didn't have time to put on a belt this morning, and you not only fall and shatter the gate, sending bite-size chards of sharp plastic flying about the room, but you also rip open a gash in your leg as you fall, but you can't react because you're thinking only of trying to get your body under the baby so she doesn't split her head open, making matters even worse, and now you have to try to calm down two wailing children before you can attempt to restore the gate and find the chards before the danger-sniffing baby turns them into a morning nosh, when all you really want to do is crawl to the bathroom to wash out the wound that feels like the Devil just took an orange zester to your shinbone, and there are still officially two hours before nap time and did I mention that you got no sleep last night, and your wife's flight won't be in until after the kids' bedtime, and your toddler is on a protest strike, refusing to sleep or even behave until she sees Mommy again—when keeping your children alive means simply protecting them from *you*.

You have to keep it together, not snap and hurl yourself into the teeth of the saber-toothed tiger outside the cave—or inside your head—even when you've had no sleep and the world is coming down around you.

If you succeed in that one thing, keeping your offspring and yourself alive until your wife gets home, do not diminish your achievement. Indeed you have every reason to be proud. You have earned your title. And a beer, I'd say.

Well done, Captain Dad.

Jargon

Every year or two, some jamoke crunches the numbers on how much a stay-at-home parent's work would be worth in the professional world, as if being a stay-at-home parent is like any other job. Well, first of all, it's not, because there is no amount you could pay me to do this work if these were not my own kids. But, that aside, if anybody truly wants this job to have the same credibility as any other, there is one thing sorely missing: jargon.

Every line of work has its own inside lingo. Every *other* line of work, that is. Part of my mission here is to change that. Toward that end, below is a starter list of terms, most of which we use around our house. Feel free to add your own and share them with other parents. Then we'll all be able to talk like pros.

Waterboarding: The last-resort technique for washing a refusenik child's hair in the kitchen sink by holding her over the counter and using the sprayer.

Mold farm: Any bathtub toy, such as a rubber duck, that has a squirter hole in it. This only allows water to be sucked inside and stay there until the black mold forms in sheets along the inner walls, making you wonder why the toy looks an oddly darker color—until you see the black bits floating in the tub, causing a queasy interruption in the bath while you drain, wash, refill the tub, and throw away the toy.

Fermenter: A diaper bin, where soiled diapers sit and grow in pungency until the bin is either filled or too foul to go another minute without emptying.

Anti-poo goo: Hand sanitizer.

"Hey, look what these can do."

Purple juice: Children's liquid acetaminophen, grape flavor.

Kidapult: A form of infant bouncy seat.

Superfriends: Comfort creatures; the stuffed animals that your kids absolutely cannot live without, the ones covered in dirt and drool and teeth marks and all other signs of a child's love.

Bungos: Someone's bottom, when you drum on it.

Germ bank: Stuffed animal, especially a superfriend.

Read-a-thon: With a stack of books and a cozy couch, it's a blissful way to wile away an hour or two in relative calm.

Diversity garden: What I call my lawn now that I have no time to take proper care of it.

Belly stampede: A hilarious bedtime stall tactic involving kids stripped to undies or a diaper and stampeding down the hall shouting, "Belly Stampeeeeeeeeeede!"

Hug party: What happens when you try to steal a moment's physical affection from your spouse, but the kids are jealous of the attention.

Booger sucker: An easier term to remember than *aspirator.*

Butt bubbles: A percussive wind from the south.

Petri dish: Any playgroup where dozens of kids slobber on all the toys. Also known as a *germ swap meet.*

CHAPTER 3

If God Had Intended Men to Carry a Child . . . She Would Have Given Us Hips

In the last chapter we talked about the equipment you will need for the job of raising a child full-time. Except I didn't cover everything. There is one other piece of equipment that is absolutely essential to your success. And guys don't have it. I know

it's beastly of me to come right out and say this, but the natural fact is indisputable, even though there is a feminist faction who would prefer it to remain unsaid. But here it is: Women are better equipped to raise children than men are. I mean physically. Equipment-wise. And I'm not talking about boobs. The equipment I speak of is lower.

I'm talking about hips. Men don't have them. Which is a debilitating disadvantage when draped all day with small children. Hips are Nature's Perch for infants and toddlers. An ever so functional ledge upon which babies the world over fit as naturally as cats on windowsills. I'm not sure if the Intelligent Design advocates have yet to glom onto this detail as proof of divine intent, but it does make you wonder why, if God had intended men to raise children, She didn't see fit to give us hips.

You see, schlepping a kid with no hips to rest her on is a real pain. I've got to do it exclusively with my manly arms. I know that men are vaunted to have superior upper-body strength, but those muscles evolved for throwing spears and opening jelly jars. Not holding wiggly lumps of baby. My Captain Dad colleagues and I may be leading Nature in a new direction, whereby men will evolve superior Baby Hoisting Power in the future, but right now we're twenty thousand years ahead of our time. And we are feeling the strain of it.

Look, it's not that I'm simply a wimp. As modern male specimens go, I may not be ripped, cut, or otherwise lacerated (if I am using the proper meathead terminology), but neither am I a total blob fish. I have above-average muscle mass and definition. For a middle-aged blob fish, at least. And let me tell you what holding a baby in the vicinity of my nonhip got me: months of excruciating pain.

It started with a twinge in my shoulder. Well, not a twinge. More of a sharp, "Holy Expletive!" sort of feeling. I would have scheduled a doctor's appointment, but that sort of luxury is for people who don't have around-the-clock child care responsibilities. Besides, we all know the scenario.

Me: "Doc, it hurts when I go like that."

Doc: "Then don't go like that."

So I tried not to "go like that." Then one night (my monthly night out, except when I can't make it because my wife is working very late) when I was sitting in a bar with the guys (we call it a writers' group, and my wife is kind enough not to challenge that charade), a sheet of paper slipped off the table. I instinctively tried to snag it out of the air like President Obama famously did with that fly in an interview. Except I did it with my bad arm.

"*Gaaah*!!" I said, for the whole bar to hear.

Everyone thought I'd been shot—the scream, the doubling over, the inability to speak for several minutes afterward. Only the absence of blood prevented someone from calling 911. Eventually I assured my colleagues with a series of grunts approximating speech that I had not, in fact, been shot. I was sure of this myself, because being shot wouldn't have hurt so much. One of the guys asked if I had seen a doctor.

My wife had been suggesting a doctor for months, but I had been shrugging it off with my good shoulder. When I got home

"Let's see, where should Jerry hurt today?"

that night and related the incident, she did her best to suppress the I-told-you-so look, which I thought was sensitive on her part. She generously carved time out of her schedule when she could stay home with the baby to allow me the chance to see a doctor, which was also sensitive. Then she truly pegged the sensitivitometer. She hooked me up with a big-shot specialist in sports medicine. Not geriatric care. Not rheumatology. But sports medicine. That's like saying, "You're not a frail old blob fish. You're a virile young stallion." Yes, I thought, a virile young stallion. Who just happened to get his keister whipped by a twenty-pound baby girl.

The sports doctor quickly sized up the problem and laid out two possible cures. One, he could cut me open and fix the problem surgically, which would require about two years' recovery time. Or, two, he could send me to physical therapy, which would require only—pay close attention now—*about two years' recovery time.*[1]

Having a good head for math, I rapidly calculated that recovery time would *not* be the deciding factor.

But time itself is always a factor. So I asked about the scheduling of surgery versus physical therapy. It turned out that I could schedule the physical therapist for early in the morning, before my daughter (we had just one then) woke up and my wife went to work. Surgery, on the other hand, would have to be scheduled during normal working hours.

Thus began my next round of considerations: Did I want months of agonizingly early mornings . . . or should I try to schedule something during the day? It was a tough call—until the doctor mentioned one last little tidbit. Surgery would *also* require months of follow-up physical therapy. The exact same amount of time as without surgery, in fact. Which makes you wonder why the heck he brought up surgery in the first place. Did he figure I was in the market for a macho scar, or did he simply have his eye on a Mediterranean villa and was a few tens of thousands short on his down payment? It's hard to say.

....

1 This proved to be a hoax. It took *four* years to get full mobility back.

Ultimately the cool scar was not sufficient enticement to endure the scheduling hassle. So off I trundled to the lair of the physical therapists.

I had never been to physical therapy before, so I didn't know what I was in for. Oh, sure, I knew there would be exercises and maybe even a big ball to bounce on, but I didn't *really* know anything about it. Had I had the foresight to check Wikipedia first, I might have learned that physical therapy developed as a by-product of the Spanish Inquisition. A windfall for the Church, really. Like a legitimate business that grows out of a front for the Mob. Anyway, some mid-level Inquisitor happened to notice one day, after releasing a victim from the rack, that the victim's posture had improved. He dutifully passed the insight up the chain of command to his abbot, who tucked it away as an alternative fund-raising idea in case that new "bingo" thing didn't work out.

Fortunately, modern physical therapy has changed dramatically since the days of the Inquisition. For one thing, it no longer takes place in a dank, dark dungeon. Instead it happens in a fluorescently lit strip mall. And for another thing, they now charge you for the experience.

Everything else—the instruments, the techniques, the dogmatic zeal—remains the same. I know I'm supposed to tag on some sort of joke here that goes, "Except such and such," but a) it's not a laughing matter, and b) there really is no freaking difference!

The condition Dr. Sports Doctor diagnosed me with is called adhesive encapsulitis, familiarly known as "frozen shoulder." It's

— Then —

— Now —

not really frozen. You *could* move it if you wanted to. And if you were a masochist. But everything that is rational in you says not to. And that's when the cycle of badness begins.

Indeed my comedy training had betrayed me: The doctor joke was all wrong.

Me: "Doc, it hurts when I go like that."

Real Doctor: "Go like that again. Again. Again. Please stop screaming. But—again . . ."

Not moving the shoulder, which you would think would be a "good" idea because you don't want to pierce your family's eardrums, turns out to be a "bad" idea. Bad. Bad, bad, bad. Your shoulder tightens up internally from the lack of stretching. Hence, the shrieking point occurs a lot sooner in any subsequent movement. And so you move your shoulder even less. And it tightens up even more. And the shrieking point . . . you get the picture.

Now that my shrieking point had shriveled to the point where mere breathing could inflict Torquemadan torture, I had to go visit one of Torquemada's latter-day disciples to have my encapsulitis unadhesed. The hardware store enthusiast in me[2] kept asking, "They make solvents for every other adhesive, even Super Glue; why not this?" Or, "What about WD-40 injections?"

But no. Three times a week I trudged over to the strip mall at the break of dawn to get thrown into a hammerlock, while fit and youthful therapists took side bets on when my eyes would pop out. My therapist was a cheery, round-faced guy named Bernie who performed musical theater at night. He couldn't

....

2 Proof: My first date with my wife was a trip to Home Depot; true story.

wait for opening night of Andrew Lloyd Webber's *Marquis De Sade!*

After an hour of his auditioning for the title role, I would slither home a broken man. My wife would size up the look on my face and ask, "How much did it hurt today, Sweetie? On a scale of nine to ten?" There had to be a better way.

A Better Way

The thought gnawed at me, not unlike the pain. "We put a man on the moon," I grumbled to myself, "but we can't make a man with hips?" Suddenly came my "aha moment." I could move to the moon, where the gravity is lower! Why, I could hold a baby all day!

Okay, maybe that specific idea was a little impractical. But the *general* idea was spot on. Invent something! That's what men do when faced with life's tough problems, don't they? And perhaps my lack of hips was merely God's way of letting me assert my manly superiority in inventing things.

Men are the world's greatest inventors, after all. What? Dare you doubt?

Ask yourself: Did a woman invent the voice-activated toilet seat? No! *Would* a woman invent even a single golf bag accessory? Hardly. Inventing stuff, even pointless stuff, is what *men* do. What woman in her right mind would ever sit down and think, "Hmm . . . here's an idea. Viagra!" I rest my case. So, maybe God foresaw the evolution of the species even to the point of male parents staying home to raise the children. Thus, She equipped men mentally to compensate for that which She did not equip us physically.

We have all heard women complain that men are not able to multitask. And I hate to spoil their fun in mocking our ways, but traditional male tasks were never as conducive to multitasking. Think about it. There was a word for the saber-tooth tiger hunter who multitasked: *meat*. For the multitasking chainsaw operator: *stumpy*. Manly tasks have historically required laser-like focus, even before the invention of the laser, which itself was invented to compensate for our biological inability to blow stuff up with our eyes. The myth that women are born geniuses at multitasking is due in large part to their ability to accomplish any number of chores with an infant parked on their hips. Well, *la ti dah*. I could do that too if I had a hip. But I don't. I have instead the manly gift of invention.

So.

Behold: the male hip extension thingy. This gizmo should make me a millionaire.

Only one obstacle remains between me and my millions: a name. Yes, if only I had a marketable moniker—the Do-It-YourShelf?—it would be like bags of cash were simply lying there on the sidewalk waiting for someone to come along and stuff his pockets. That someone being me. The Hipster? Sidecar Baby? The technology will be easy. My R&D dollars will be best spent on marketing. The Hip-Hopper? Reconstructive Shoulder Surgery Saver? Come on, help me out here. You have ideas? Shout 'em out. Something catchy and dot-com-able, please.

Until I come up with a million-dollar name, alas, the Baby-Bench will never materialize, which means that I have to find another way to support my children. On my body, that is.

The obvious choice when the girls were itty-bitty was the baby carrier known variously as the Baby Bjorn, Snuggli, or Kangaroo Helper. It is the easiest of options for hands-free baby transport. But it is not without its drawbacks. For one thing, the baby is on your chest and can reach almost anything in front of you that you can. God forbid you should try to eat anything. And if God won't forbid it, the baby certainly will. Babies just love grabbing things. Not just food, either. It could be any old thing: a paring knife, a steaming tea kettle, the toaster oven grill.

Nevertheless, Grabby Hands of Death notwithstanding, this modern baby carrier remains a useful object. Up to a point. That point is when the baby's legs get long enough to . . . how do I put this?

You see, with this type of baby carrier, the baby's legs hang straight down. Straight. Down. And babies of a certain age—particularly the age when their legs get a little longer—they, um . . . they like to kick. And . . .

Oh, please tell me I don't have to spell it out.

Look, if your personal standard equipment came with manly bits instead of girly bits, and if you have any ambitions for a larger family—or you simply don't want to have to explain to your older children why Daddy is collapsed on the ground squeaking like a Betsy Wetsy doll—then you may want to retire the kangaroo pack by the time the baby reaches a year old.

Then what? Well, there are backpacks, of course, but you can't sit down anywhere with them. That, and they tend to be pretty bulky and hard to toss into the car with all the other Infant Transport Material you need these days.

So I was pleased to discover an older technology that still works, even for men. It is called "cloth." Yes, the same cloth that "clothes" are made of, only with stylish Third World patterns woven into it, to remind others of your appreciation of the Old

Wisdom of Ancient Cultures (not counting their traditional gender roles).

Now, for the gadget-happy modern Western male, this ancient cloth thingy might be a little disconcerting, and not merely because it can't be patented and exploited for millions of dollars (by me, of course). But, you see, a woman likely invented this particular technology. It's cloth, after all. And the knots it uses aren't complicated enough to warrant a Cub Scout merit badge.

Still, one can't help but to marvel at the way, when you use it to strap your child to your chest, the child's legs are splayed wide, as if those ancient women inventors were considering the future of the species. Little feet may kick madly at the air or even graze that boyish little pelvis of yours. But your knickered bits go blissfully unknackered.

As an extra super-special bonus, when the baby is not loaded in your cloth sling, the crisscrossed draping gives you a cool "bandolero" look. *¡Es muy macho!* Not that you're looking to hit on nannies or anything, but something in a guy's lizard brain always appreciates a little bravado. No matter how little. Or delusional.

Like thinking you look cool in a baby sling.

Okay, so it's not cool. It is, rather, unhip. But that's my whole problem. I am unhipped. So I am totally cool with wearing an overgrown Third World hippie scarf invented by a woman . . . so long as it spares me from nut-cracking babies and shoulder-cracking physical therapists.

Wear a cup. It's not just the front-loading baby carriers you need to be afraid of. You'll be on the phone with the gas company, carefully repeating your account number for the eleventh time, utterly oblivious to the affectionate toddler barreling toward you like a waist-high bullet train. Or you'll be stealing a moment's respite, on your back on the floor in the playroom, when a thirty-pound giggling cannon ball drops out of the sky. Or you'll be tucking your sweet little angel into bed when she swings around in a volley of elbows and knees because she absolutely has to have one more hug.

The next instant, you are feeling something relatively low on your anatomy trying to leap out through the back of your neck.

The front of the average guy makes a target area of roughly nine square feet. The most vulnerable part of that is just a few square inches. But what do you think the kids manage to connect with every time? Bingo. Rather, *bango clango, owie kazowie*!

If you think I am in any way exaggerating, just watch any episode of *America's Funniest Home Videos.* You'll see at least twenty crotchings—and those were only the ones both caught on video that week and deemed interesting enough or severe enough for national airtime. They built a television empire based on the predictability of these collisions. Taking a shot to the crotch is *de rigueur* for any dad with small kids. And a stay-at-home dad is with his kids at least five times as much as other dads. Perhaps that is why cave women organized primitive society the way they did: "Honey, if this species is going to survive, maybe *you* should go out and hunt the big fearsome animals while I tend to the *little* fearsome animals."

The only possible up side to having my testicles mutilated in a parenting-related incident is that the subsequent loss of whatever testosterone I have left may slow my hair loss. I admit that that is a tempting trade-off.

But, nah. I think I'll stick with the less painful option. I have already snared a mate to provide offspring; I don't need my hair anymore anyway.

CHAPTER 4

What's All This I Hear About Sleep Deprivation?

Captain Dad is not just some self-aggrandizing title; it's a self-aggrandizing *movement.* We stay-at-home dads are rising up to . . . well . . . do . . . something. Or other. We're not really sure just what at the moment. We're too sleep deprived to think straight right now. The stay-at-home moms are the only ones who can probably understand this, but they don't particularly have the energy to care. So I don't know why I even brought this up. Except perhaps to say . . .

I need to start drinking coffee. I really do. My problem is that I didn't start young enough. I know, how hard could it be to start drinking coffee? But think about it. Coffee is more than a drink; it's a ritual. There is a process involved, a certain sophistication that lets you discern a "good" cup of coffee from a "bad" one. Being able to recognize good cups and bad cups is a very important part of coffee drinking, from what I can tell. I don't think I could find the time to cultivate such a sophistication, let alone ritualism. I barely have time to water the plants; and when I say barely, I mean I barely have time to water them every two or three weeks instead of once a week like I ought to. And people ask why we don't have pets. It's hard enough explaining the plants. Imagine the desiccated husk of a cat toppling off the stoop in a cloud of dander. I'd have the animal rights people on my doorstep in a heartbeat, and I'd have to be out there spouting some claptrap about Darwin's survival of the fluffiest and saying, "Sorry, can't talk now, the baby's crying for—I don't know, water?" And that would just bring on Family Services, if they could bully their way through the animal rights protesters, and—What was I saying? Oh, yeah.

Does Starbucks deliver?

Sleep deprivation is real. You hear women all the time talking about how the baby stole their brain cells, and I swear it's because of lost sleep. And the multitasking. And the never-below-Yellow-Alert stress. Clinical studies show that these three factors can lower your cognitive capability, and you know that these studies are credible because they are conducted by unmarried graduate students who don't have children to lower their cognitive capabilities. Having children makes you dumber, and it's not simply due to the level of conversation.

Daughter: "Why is it white?"

Me: "What, the cloudy sky?"

Daughter: "No, bird poop."

Your IQ drops as much as 10 percent. That's what the studies say, anyway.

Being a guy, however, I had the macho not-me attitude. A *man* would be too tough to be cerebrally neutered by a tyke. So I got tested. And I *proved* it. Unfortunately, I proved the child-free scientists' thesis, not my own. Almost to the decimal point. Only 90 percent of my gray cells are now firing on all cylinders. Okay,

brain cells may not have cylinders, but what do I know? I've lost 10 percent of my brain! If this trend continues until my kids are off to school all day, I won't be qualified to go back and get work as a greeter at Walmart.

So, for now at least, someone else is going to have to split the atom. I am preoccupied with other, more volatile pursuits. Like splitting a bag of Goldfish crackers between two toddlers without triggering a meltdown that makes Chernobyl look like a hissy fit.

Sleep deprivation doesn't begin when the baby is born. It begins the moment your wife's belly gets too big for her to sleep comfortably. You may go a few nights before you notice it, but if you continue to get a good night's sleep while she is tossing next to you, that will change if she kicks you down to the couch. So bite the bullet, lie awake, rub her back or something. Years down

"Why couldn't we have gotten the one with the snooze button?"

the road you won't remember the sleep you lost. Or else she'll remember it forever.

Once the baby comes, it gets much, much worse . . . or so I vaguely remember. The brain is too exhausted to etch those years into one's long-term memory. Hence the wisdom of baby scrapbooks and home videos; you can go back later and reconstruct your memories.

I do remember bragging, however, "The baby's only two weeks old and I can honestly claim to have gotten eight hours of sleep. And I hope to get another eight over the *next* two weeks." With the second child it was worse, of course. Especially once my wife went back to work and I was flying solo with the kids. I retired at the end of the day with a Do Not Resuscitate order slapped across my chest.

Lack of Sleep Makes You Crazy

You ever wonder where kids get so much energy? I'll tell you. They get it from their parents. They suck it out of us like little mosquitoes. I'd say vampires, but vampires are very chic these days, and that might somehow make having the life sucked out of you seem attractive. So let's stick with mosquitoes. Constantly buzzing about you, wanting to be fed (okay, okay, all you sticklers, even part brain-dead I know that the mosquitoes that suck your blood are not the ones that buzz, but just work with me here). They want to be fed or changed, or wiped, or answered, or given attention in any way imaginable. Or unimaginable. So you'd think that at the end of the day, you'd simply collapse into a deep unconsciousness. You wish! But how can anyone sleep with twenty-five-pound mosquitoes in the house?

A child's need for attention never sleeps. Not a week goes by without a bedtime bellyache, which, after some probing questions, seems to be radiating from the elbow. Or a middle-of-the-night "bad dream" that sounds curiously like a book we just read. And the description of their invented maladies always ends with, "You need to sleep in *my* room tonight," or, "Move over. I need to sleep in *your* bed." The problem is, it's not *always* a ploy. So my ability to rest restfully is shot to pieces. My unconscious ear is conscientiously scanning the airwaves for sounds of distress—a kid falling out of bed, retching with violent illness, crying out from a bona fide scary dream. Any kind of sound—a real-life mosquito farts two doors down—and I'm bolt upright, veins awash in adrenaline. You hear about Green Berets who come home after prolonged combat duty and are like this. They've learned to anticipate danger and spring from their sleeping bags, in full combat gear, weapon reassembled, bayonets in their teeth—all in less than one second. They'd make great Captain Dads, whatever their rank in the military. They have the requisite instincts to be the go-to parent in a household.

Of course, they usually come home and check into the VA to lose those instincts, which are more commonly known as combat fatigue syndrome. Me, I don't get to call my condition a syndrome, but just between you and me, I think I'm just as loco.

I do. I hallucinate and everything. I hear the Phantom Fish Box. Even when the kids are away visiting grandparents, I hear it in the duct work. *Bum, bum-bum, bum-bum, bum-bum . . .*

The Fish Box is a little music box that hangs over the crib rail or bed headboard. It has a cute underwater scene and a nice big button the kids can smack to play soothing music if they can't sleep or simply want a reassuring glow and sound of bubbles. Something in the overtones of the white noise in the duct work makes me hear it in the middle of the night and worry what the distress might be. But I don't want to get out of bed and inquire and wake up an otherwise sleeping child.

So I lie awake, straining my ears to tell if it's the real Bum-Bum Fish or the Phantom Fish Box. And the sleep minutes trickle away.

Yellow Alert. You never dip below it, even when you sleep.

Well, almost never. I do recall, on at least two separate occasions, the guiltless pleasure of having gone to bed without remembering to turn on the baby monitor and sleeping deeply all the way until daylight—for once—and wondering why I had gotten such an uninterrupted, and shockingly restful, night's sleep. What a wonderful feeling! It was a restfulness that I was literally able to enjoy for minutes after waking. Two, three, possibly even several. Then I was racing for a bottle to quell the screams, and chasing down rogue socks that seem to have replaced dust bunnies as the bane of our housekeeping.

But sleep deprivation isn't all fun and games. It has its darker moments. One of our daughters went through an unfortunate phase in her first year.[3] She would go through three or four, or five or six, diapers in a single change. Even though she was pretty good at sleeping through the night, I remember one particularly bleak two o'clock in the morning when she was having diaper trouble. This was maybe six months into the gaping sleep void known as the child's first year.

A Case Study

So I shuffle into my daughter's room. I open the diaper. There's poop. Bear in mind that this little girl must have been a dung beetle in a previous life, the way she objects to having her diapers changed. I start the changing. It's not clumpy poop—it's poo balls. They start rolling around. One rolls out. I grab it with a wipe. Her dung beetle soul starts channeling bucking bronco spirits to help her register her protest, as I try to hold the feet of this possessed, writhing body. Poo balls are rolling all over and soiling the clean diaper I had laid under her. I grab another clean diaper, hold it in my teeth while I try to move away the two defiled ones—a precarious gambit that means two or three seconds of exposed changing table. Luckily I lay the new diaper down just in time to catch the second surge of poop. It's not poo balls this time

....

3 Note to any daughter of ours who may read this when she is older: It wasn't you, it was your sister.

"Everybody says it goes by quickly. It better."

but a seething wall of magma. I need yet another diaper. While I'm reaching for it, I realize that the lava stream is not stopping. This new diaper will, at best, catch the overflow of "number two" in clean diaper number three. Of course, that's if I can slide it in under diaper number two in time. More luck, I succeed and there comes a break in the action, which I know better than to expect might be the end of it all. So I fold over the two latest victims of insult and overlay them with a fourth clean diaper. I stand and

stare blankly at the wall for a moment as if drumming mental fingers. No need to wonder what is coming next. Like an exhale follows an inhale. And, sure enough, one more diaper down. But I have developed a feel for this over the months (something I may put on my résumé under "Special Skills") and this one has an air of finality about it. At last. Since it is the middle of the night, I have the lights on low, so I don't really know the extent of the casualties, but it appears that I have stacked the serial dirty diapers without smearing anything on the dresser, and I think I've likewise managed to preserve the chastity of the changing-table pad—thus far. So it rationally ignites the flicker of hope in me that I will be able to return to bed very soon now. I dig around in the basket on the shelf below the changing table for clean diaper number five. Crap! I'm out of diapers! The next closest clean one is nearly eight feet away on the other side of the room. What do I do? How the hell do *I* know what to do—*I'm missing part of my brain and it's the middle of the night!* I fold over part of the latest poo-bogged diaper, so as to cushion her bum on something not entirely disgusting, and lunge for the box of back-ups, calculating that if the bucking beetle rolls off the table, I'll still be able to slide a foot under her to break her fall, and, saints be praised, it works. The baby is alive, on the table, and I find in my hand three clean diapers as the prize of my blind grab. Best of all, very little poo has been squished up the baby's back. I should be able to wrap this up with only three or four wipes, an estimate that proves accurate. Now I have only to swap out the mountain of soiled diapers for a clean one, and I can pop her back in her sleep sack before popping back into my own.

That's when the pee fountain begins. The cover on the changing table pad is lost. Ditto the pajamas. Hers and mine.

And the baby starts to scream.

Suddenly it makes sense to me how I could read in the paper about the horrible things people do to sweet, innocent babies. I keep my own name out of the headlines, somehow, because there is that wispy thread of God knows what holding me back, keeping me (just barely) civilized in the face of feral frustration. But I understand. And I don't judge those notoriously bad parents as harshly. I only hurt for them. And thank God for whatever it is that I've been given that they have lost.

Then, once I move all the scatologically tainted wreckage from the scene, hastily clean my hands with wipes and anti-poo goo, and wrangle her distraught little body into dry jammies, I hug my baby until she stops crying. I put her in her sack, lay her in her crib, and slip away to clean myself off. Then I lie down in my own bed, silently sobbing so as not to wake my wife and torture her dreams with my sleep-deprived waking nightmares.

But I Can't Complain—or Else!

Undoubtedly someone will judge me harshly for even contemplating sympathy for those horrid parents. But I'll bet it's someone with a job outside the home.

I mean, let's say you work a regular job. You may love what you do, but aren't there ever days when you want to chuck it all? Days that are simply too aggravating to endure in a good mood? Maybe a coworker drives you crazy. Or it's a Dilbertian boss, or a subordinate, or a client. Or the work itself. It can be physically exhausting or emotionally exhausting or both. And on a Friday night when you get together with friends and coworkers, you just might blow off steam in a way that could be interpreted as having a negative attitude toward your job. But it's okay because everyone gets it, everyone understands, or feels the same.

That's the great thing about work. You can love it and hate it at the same time—or hate it and hate it at the same time—and you'll always find an understanding ear and a sympathetic song on the radio. Not so with raising a kid. No matter how aggravating the day may be, no matter how emotionally and physically and spiritually—and any otherwisely—exhausted you may be, there is no level on which you can express anything other than love for the job, or you will be demonized beyond your worst

imagining. "Even Hitler loved his dog!" That's how bad it will be. Someone will cite Hitler.

So you offer a vacant, some would say psychotic, smile and garble a bromide such as, "Yes, it's exhausting, but it's a good tired," and everyone politely ignores the hunted look in your eye. And is glad that they get to go to work instead.

Nights-and-weekends parents don't want to know how hard it is. They are happy to complain about long hours or being on the road and imagine themselves martyrs, admired for their fortitude and grit; but offer them the chance to turn the tables and be the one home with the kids during their spouses' prolonged absences, and you're in for an entertaining tap dance. Like my next-door neighbor who, after a ten-day business trip, came home to his wife and three kids under the age of four—just long enough to grab his golf clubs.

These types of parents, by the way, are always the ones with the great advice for us full-timers on what to do in any given situation. Something they read in the in-flight magazine, no doubt.

Okay, you may not want to read this part to your husband if you're hoping to sell him on taking the plunge into Captain Dad–hood. But if you're the stay-at-home mom, either hoping to switch spots or hoping to hang on, just know that there is a man out there who gets it. A very, very tired man, who takes all of those dark thoughts and tucks them away in the 10 percent of his brain that he may never get back. Hmm, maybe sleep deprivation isn't all bad.

They're So Perfect When They Sleep

My first daughter was born a little after eight in the evening. My wife and I had started that day near dawn, timing contractions and loading up to head to the hospital. So when the momentous day and night finally wound down around eleven, and we were free to sleep (or try, at least)—my wife in her hospital bed, me on the foldout foam couch in her room, and our adorable new baby in her molded plastic cradle-on-a-cart—I could barely stand.

But I had to. There was one more thing I had to do.

On wobbly legs, with shaky hands, I scratched out a sketch of our firstborn, barely three hours into this world and bundled like a burrito. Until my energy gave out altogether. Even with her nose mashed from living in a constrained womb for so long (it fluffed out to symmetrical in a couple of weeks), she was unbearably beautiful. And perfect.

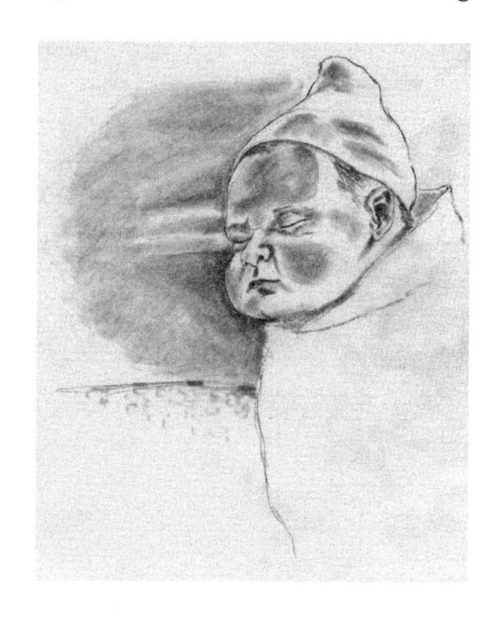

When I collapsed after my drawing, however, neither my wife nor I could actually sleep. We could only stare in wonder at the little subject, listening to her tiny breaths. It was

probably near three in the morning before exhaustion shut our eyes for us.

You would think that we would have learned since then to steal every moment of sleep we can to keep up with them, especially on those days when they are absolutely, exasperatingly insane. But we still can't help ourselves sometimes from sneaking into their room to stand and watch. And I still try once in a while to capture their slumbering forms on paper by the shabby glimmer of the nightlight.

Because, even with their legs hanging off the bed, their arms flopped everywhere, their little bodies lost among their menageries and tangled blankets, I get to see them the way they truly are. Perfect.

At least, when they sleep.

CHAPTER 5

Top Ten Tattletale Clues to a Captain Dad's Secret Identity (Even without Kids)

Let's say you see a man on the street, in a bar, at a reception for the Latvian General Consul (*could* happen), passing himself off as an ordinary adult. Ever wonder if he could be a superhero with a secret identity? You do? Well, hmm. Maybe you've read too many comic books.

If you're not a comic book reader, however, then you might not have this particular curiosity because you're not quite sure what clues to look for. For instance, you might see a Captain Dad blending in with a crowd because his children are momentarily at his mother-in-law's house and he has a couple of hours to himself to remember what it used to be like to be a carefree adult. You might see him and think, *Hey, there goes that not-so-famous architect.* Or that journeyman plumber. Or that barista who knows everything about every episode of *Battlestar Gallactica*.

Until you notice the barf on his lapel—something you would never have thought to look for. At least, not until the first Captain Dad comic boo—er, *graphic novel* hits the bookstores (*Captain Dad vs. the Sticky Fingers of Doom,* Issue #1).

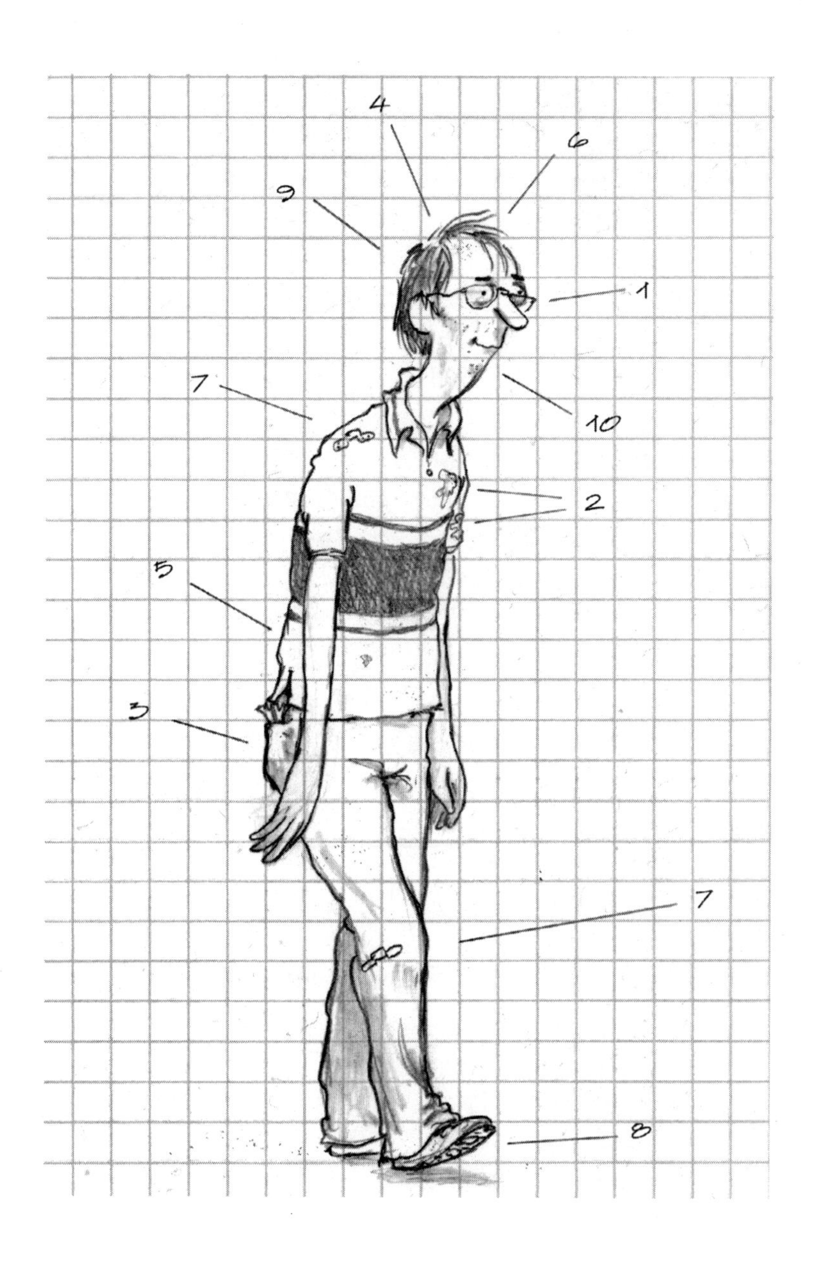
4
6
9
1
7
10
2
5
3
7
8

Until then, you can use this secret decoder map to spot these new American heroes.

1. Bent glasses. Had I had the good sense to have kids at a more conventional age, middle age would not yet have savaged my near vision. And I would not have to wear the reading glasses that basically amount to a target on my face. Kids have a knack for smacking your glasses in the most adorably painful ways. It's the pogo jump just when you bend over to pick them up. The wildly flailing hands that never need a reason to flail. The rogue heel trying to evade your grasp while you are changing a particularly messy diaper. Ultimately it was a simple head butt from the squirmal in my arms that snapped the cord holding my lens and sent me trotting off to the eye doctor's office. I explained what happened the best I could, but the cumulative damage to my frames left me with zero credibility. The receptionist gleefully relayed to me the technician's indignant rebuttal: "He totally sat on these!" I'm guessing that he does not have kids of his own.

Oh, and let's not forget the other fun game with glasses. A two-year-old whose fingers are age-appropriately sticky thinks it's hilarious to give you simulated cataracts by smearing them all over your lenses. I tried explaining to mine that I am a professional humorist and I know funny . . . and that ain't funny. She just laughed.

2. Yogurt stains. Yogurt stains can be wiped off eyeglasses relatively easily, but they have a way of making themselves indelible on clothing. Unlike many other food stains, which can be rinsed right out in the sink, these only tend to spread out and leave a bigger blot than before. But you can't avoid yogurt. It is one of those rare semi-healthy foods that kids will actually eat. And once they reach the age where they realize how messy it can be, they will *demand* it. That's typically the age when they start feeding themselves. And yogurt is something that even the youngest toddler will demand on spooning (or fingering) onto his or her own face. Sometimes even into his or her own mouth. So what do you do about those icky yogurt hands afterward? You try to wipe them, that's what you do. But, here's the catch. Most kids have two—count 'em—two hands. And you need one of your hands to hold one of their hands while you wipe it with your other hand. Do the math. We have one hand unaccounted for. One very yogurty little hand. What's it doing? Look at your shirt.

The only good thing about yogurt stains is that there are other stains that can pass for yogurt. So if someone asks what that drool, snot, or spit-up is on your shirt, just say, "Yogurt. Of course!"

3. Diaper bulge in pocket. Packing a spare clean diaper at all times does leave you with an unsightly bulge, but don't leave home without it or you'll quickly learn where the acronym SOL came from.

4. Glitter. I'll be walking my daughter down the aisle someday and notice the glint of something stuck to her scalp. Something that shouldn't be there. Guess what it will be. Glitter. From a My Little Pony she had when she was three! Which we threw out when she was four (and told her that the glitter meant it was

A SPARE
NUMBER THREE?
ANYONE?
A THREE...
TWO?... FOUR?..
ANYONE?

magic, so it had to go and save the pixies in Magic Land). If I get a zit, the first thing I have to do is make sure that it's not just glitter blocking my pores.

What full-blooded nitwit ever thought it was a bright idea to tart up toys with toxic waste? Oh, to have been a fly (a tsetse fly!) on the wall in the meeting where they came up with that.

"Ooh! Ooh! I have an idea! Let's cover these toys with tiny shards of shiny material."

"That's genius! What will attach it to the toy?"

"Attach it? Can't we just hold enough of it in place until the kid gets the toy out of the box, and then who cares what happens to it?"

"Give that man a raise!"

But it's not just on toys, it's on greeting cards and the waistbands of underpants. It's in glue and crayons. And clothes! Yikes, one dress-up princess dress can spangle your house with enough glitter to declare an environmental emergency.

5. Stooped walk. If I were my own mother, I'd nag myself to stand up straight. But I can't. I mean, physically I can. But responsibly I can't. All my daily duties happen down in short-person space. Tending children is a lot like being a shortstop. His back would feel much better if he stood straight up in the field, but he would miss all the important plays. Unlike a shortstop, however, my inning never ends.

6. Rapidly thinning hair. My wedding pictures show me with a luxuriant mop of silken locks. "Yikes!" you would say. "What woman *wouldn't* marry a head of hair like that!" At least, that's how I like to imagine it, ignoring the throngs of women who found me resistible in the decades before that photo. No matter. I had hair. And I have the pictures to prove it. Even in the picture of me holding my firstborn for the first time, there was something definitely covering my head, something apparently organic in origin.

Some of the blame clearly falls on the kids, who love to pull on daddy's hair to see what funny faces he will make. ("*Eek! Aaaggh! Ow! Ooochi!*") Another reason could be that the "product" I use in my hair tends to be products you'd find in the snack or dairy aisle of the supermarket, again thanks to wandering sticky little fingers.

But I'm guessing that most of the loss is due to some biological switch being thrown. The DNA Systems Manager in my brain sent out the memo to all my scalp cells that read, "Lose the hair. Cut off his other breeding options and keep the family safe by dumping them silken locks." Somehow none of them bothered to notice the dearth of women who wanted me *with* hair. Since I have no interest in breaking up the family so I can go back to being a lonely sad sack for another few decades, can't I at least keep a few follicles for my wife's benefit? Did it ever occur to my DNA that *she* might like my hair? How about *that* as a family preservation issue!

Overheard on the Playground:
"Da-a-ad! Braden won't let me touch the slug!"

7. Band-Aids on his clothes. I blame this on women in the workforce. Some working mom at the Johnson & Johnson company must have hit on a brainwave one day. Her kids had just decorated their coloring books with some pretty stickers. Square stickers with perforated edges. And funny little numbers and the words, "First Class." After wondering what ever possessed the Post Office to get rid of the cheaper-to-produce lick-and-stick stamps for the peel-and-stick variety, it suddenly dawned on her. The Post Office just reaped a $40 windfall due to the wasted stamps. Kids don't know or care that stamps aren't really stickers. They have pretty pictures and they stick to things. To them, that's a sticker. *Hmm . . .* she thought. *What else sticks, is not a sticker, but could be made to look like one enough to guarantee plenty of wasted product?* She waltzed into the office the next day with the thought of printing pictures of Scooby Doo, Sponge-Bob, or the Disney Princesses on Band-Aids. Within a week, bandage sales charts couldn't have been better if there had been a global leprosy epidemic. And that astute working mom never gave a care about losing sticky stamps again. Heck, she can now wallpaper her house with them.

And why not? *Our* house was wallpapered with those bandages. Walls, floors, the kids' clothes. Especially their pajamas. They went to bed looking like King Tut. And some of those bandages were really tough to get off. Wash after wash, they'd cling to those PJs, eventually bonding entirely with the fabric. And do you know what was truly pathetic? We'd go out and buy *more* bandages. It turned out that they were actually cheaper than the fancy stickers in the greeting card aisle.

8. Stickers on the soles of his shoes. It may not be as glamorous as the Paul Simon song of a similar name, but it is just as much a defining quality of our central character. Non–Band-Aid stickers don't stick as stickily as Band-Aids do. It is supposed to be a selling point that the adhesive on modern stickers will not stick permanently to things like furniture, walls, heirlooms, and so on. And for this consideration, parents everywhere are eternally grateful. The down side is that your children's stickers—which come in books of one thousand so they will provide an entire afternoon's fun—fall off of whatever they have been originally stuck to and end up on the floor. Until you step on them. Then somehow those stickers stick just fine to the soles of your shoes.

9. "The Wheels on the Bus Go Round and Round." All through the town. That's what you may find us unconsciously humming. We only listen to kid-friendly music. Not that we wouldn't love to listen to anything—anything! But surprisingly few grown-up songs, even bubble-gum pop from days of yore, slip by without raising uncomfortable questions in a curious five-year-old who tries to memorize every song she hears. My wife is only a few years younger than me, but her tween years had the misfortune of falling in the rise of disco, so she likes music with a good beat, but she has learned never to listen to the lyrics too hard (a necessary skill if you want to enjoy disco). She was broadcasting music from her iPod throughout the kitchen one day, when I asked her what this song was about. She said, "Not to worry, all they say is [whatever dance hook line it was]." She had never really listened to it. But *I* was listening. And I'm only glad my daughters didn't hear [whatever horrifying lyrics] before I was able to drop some dishes as a distraction while I lunged for the stop button. So. The wheels on the bus go round and round. All through your head.

10. Halfway between Hollywood and Skidrow stubble. "Daddy! I want milk!" "Daddy! Don't shave. We're playing doctor. You need to be my patient." "Daddy! Poop alert! Poop alert!" A Captain Dad's unevenly shaved face does not scream, "I *meant* not to shave today, thank you very much." As if he expects a paparazzo to pop out of the bushes and snap his picture. Nor does it look hopelessly neglected. It has a subtler, interrupted quality to it. As if he *meant* to shave, but breakfast was an endless run of "I'm still hungry!" and there were still some dishes left over from the night before that had to be cleaned, and then there was sweeping, and more sweeping after the last "I'm still hungry" resulted in rye toast, and there was still a lunch to get ready for school, and the little one needed changing—twice—and his wife had to leave for work early, and oh my goodness look at the clock you've got to be in school quick get on your shoes! Shoes! SHOES! And . . .

But if you want to think it's a Hollywood shave, and that I'm not a secret hero but a movie star (albeit an aging one with thinning hair), that's okay, too.

Who's the Hero?

Are modern parents the Great American Heroes we make ourselves out to be? Do we really have it harder than any prior generation, even with all our modern conveniences? I'm not one to speculate. No, let's let the facts speak for themselves.

Let's look at my grandmother. She never had to worry about running out of disposable diapers. She could just rinse one out, or pull it off the clothesline. In a real pinch, she could pin on a dish towel. But, alas, there's no chance of that today. How many times have you reached for a diaper, only to remember that you had no time to dash out to Costco for another carton, and now you have to ransack the house, your coat pockets, the diaper bag . . . for one last diaper, because it's late and only the convenience stores are open, but they'll only gouge you, and besides the kids need to be in bed? Ah, for Grandma's simpler times!

And did Grandma worry about melamine in baby formula? No way. In her day, they didn't have the agencies, let alone the technology, to test for it. Hormones in milk? Never! Nor did she worry about running out, when all she had to do was waltz out to the barn and squeeze out a pint.

And what about trying to schedule work done on the house? Grandma didn't have to juggle pre-school, soccer, ballet lessons, and summer "camps." She could always count on being at home—not that she would ever have had to worry about waiting for a plumber or a furnace repairman. She didn't need a plumber for an outhouse. And her potbelly stove never broke down. She simply had to chop some more wood, and the heat kept coming.

She didn't have to strap kids into car seats. She didn't have to make sure they wore helmets on their bicycles, tricycles, roller skates, trampolines, or sofas while playing video games. In those days people would walk out on the wing of an airplane with less protection.

There were no scary cultural villains, either, like TV or the Internet. No noisemaking toys. There were hardly any toys at all, thanks to the Great Depression. But who needed them anyway, when a stick and a barrel hoop meant hours of entertainment? Or an old rag doll. Hardly the same threat as a Barbie or a Slutz doll's precocious sexuality.

Most of all, Grandma didn't have to heap all her worries and aspirations onto one or two kids. She could spread them out over her seven children. Bliss!

But I don't mean to take anything away from her own heroism. To her it seemed like a challenge. After all, she had it twice as hard as her mother did. Her mother had sixteen children.

Hoo-wee! When you have that many kids, what's a black sheep or two?

Let us, then, strive to make sure that our own children do not have it as rough as we do. As heroes, I think it's the least we can do.

And I always try to do the least I can do.

CHAPTER 6

Man vs. Disney

I'm man enough to admit my failures. And there is no shame in succumbing to insurmountable odds. Even Superman lost a battle or two.

I had always intended to raise my children in a Disney-free household. But then, what did I know? I had no kids at the time.

The first breach came on Day One. Disposable diapers. I told myself that diaper designs didn't count. After all, both Huggies *and* Pampers were branded with Disney characters. Where else could I turn? Store brand? Cloth diapers? Biodegradables? Respectively: no, eww, and don't be ridiculous. And I'm not goofy enough to take that toilet-training-from-birth approach like those wackos in that *New York Times* article someone has inevitably e-mailed to you by now.

"To see with the eyes of a child."
Translation: To desire things with the expectation that someone else will pay for them.

At first I tried telling my daughter that the mouse on the front of her diaper was called Poopy Mouse. Being a guy, I thought it was funny. But ultimately I didn't think it was healthy for my daughter to see her mommy swatting her daddy every time he said it, so I ended up caving on calling him

Mickey. Then we switched to the diapers that featured Winnie the . . . (wait for it) Pooh! Some joker at the diaper company had to be laughing his own undies off over that one. And how could I fight it anymore? Every guy, even the steeliest opponent of licensed characters, has a weakness for cheap potty humor.

Despite this capitulation to Disneyana, we remained vigilant against any other encroachment of Mauschwitz on our home. But that was just the home front.

We could not protect our children from the magic kingdom, which they would frequently visit to become princesses all day long and feast on treats with their favorite Disney characters. Of course, I'm talking about Grammy's house.

Oops, I'm sorry. Did I use the phrase "magic kingdom?" Uh-oh, that might confuse some people to think that my mother-in-law's house was comparable in some way to Disney World. But that would be absurd. No, Grammy's house is no Magic Kingdom. It is a Magic *Empire,* of Alexander the Great proportions.

We are talking about the original Fairy Grandmother, my mother-in-law. The woman is truly magical. Even by grandmother standards she is bonkers about her grandchildren. That alone would be enough to put any child under her thrall. But we discovered another of her enchantments one day when our then-two-year-old overheard that it was Grammy on the telephone and blurted out, "Sugar? Chocolate?"

But that *still* did not explain it all. Nor did the fact that her house had way more toys in it than ours did. What accounted for the rest? What secret necromancy did Grammy's house possess that ours did not? What spell did she cast that took us three whole days to deprogram our children when they returned home from a visit to Grammy's?

One word: *cable.*

Yes, I know that it paints us as Luddite freaks not to have cable. But if we did, we'd be paying fifty or sixty bucks a month for maybe a couple of hours of viewing. Pull out the time for commercials, and that's more per minute than a Broadway show.

"When do we get past foofy dresses and into real policy issues?"

Of course, this means my wife and I had no clue about certain pop cultural issues. For example, it didn't occur to me at first what was going on when I'd keep getting asked, "Who's your favorite princess?" I was not yet aware that the Disney Princesses had formed an alliance and intended to annex all of young female America. So my replies were something in the way of blank looks. Much like my daughter's blank look the time I answered, "Um, Victoria of Sweden?"

By the time my older daughter turned four, she had become fully indoctrinated in the Princess cult. She'd arrive at the breakfast table in her Cinderella dress and her Cinderella wig—yes, wig, compliments of guess who—and I'd have to play along. "Oh, hello, Princess Cinderella. Have you seen Rebecca anywhere?" I'd say.

"Oh, no," she'd say breathily, "Rebecca must be way back in Chicago. There's no Rebecca here in Disney." Mind you, we had never been to Disney. My wife and I had not so much as acknowledged its existence. So where did she get this "here in Disney" business? Grammy's house, of course—along with a burgeoning trousseau of princess apparel.

I had lost. Between the diapers and Grammy, I was flat on the mat, with Disney doing the Rocky dance above my head. My only hope was a rematch.

Flash forward a year or so. The phone rang. Grammy. No big reason, just a routine call. Oh, and by the way, *Disney on Ice* was in town for only four more days. Casually noted. A passing thought. Hardly worth mentioning. Who knew why it even came up at all? Ho hum.

Except.

Grammy has a way of effortlessly creating a sense of urgency (the dark side of Grammy magic perhaps). I honestly cannot tell you how it happened or what exactly overcame my resistance to such an idea, but within minutes I had four seats for that Saturday's *Disney on Ice* show *Before It Left Town*. Like a robot on meth, I had dialed up tickets and was now committed to an afternoon of ice-skating princesses—before I had even processed what was going on. In my blind haste, I had ordered two extra tickets, one for my wife and one more so my daughter could bring a friend.

My wife would not want to go, but I figured it would be a fair penance. It was *her* mother who caused this. But the sins of the mother-in-law could not be visited on her daughter this time. The friend from preschool would only go if her mom could go with us.

Her mom was unable to schedule a root canal on such short notice, so the four of us were on our way to the United Center (home of the Chicago Blackhawks, by the way, whom I would *not* be seeing). Luckily we got there in time for the Princess Preshow.

We got to see Cinderella and Belle take turns walking out onto a tiny platform along the upper concourse of the stadium to smile and wave mutely at children for five minutes, then duck behind a curtain to wait their next turn and ponder the years they spent studying Shakespeare only to end up with a costumed smile-and-wave gig for three shows a day on the road.

“There’s a show on tonight that we should Tivo and watch later, when the kids have gone to college.”

My own cynical wondering about the very same was interrupted when my little princess asked me why the Cinderella on the platform didn't look like the "real" Cinderella.

"What? No!" I retorted. "She looks *exactly* like the Cinderella on your shirt. Don't you think?" At least the actress was getting paid to act.

"We failed the credit check."

Hopefully she was getting paid as much as I was paying for the tickets, parking, and cotton candy, all of which would have put her in an enviable tax bracket. I mean, the cotton candy alone was twelve dollars. Twelve. Dollars. I have written many jokes for this book. That is not one of them. Count 'em. Twelve. Cotton candy.

But I couldn't *not* buy it. Just a few weeks earlier in my daughter's preschool, the question in Small Group was posed, "Who here has had cotton candy?" Every hand went up but one. So. I rationalized it as a trivial expense, with the thought that by the time she gets to college, twelve bucks won't even cover one page of a textbook. Or five minutes worth of psychotherapy.

Anyway.

The show itself was a respectably polished piece of schlock spectacle whose only truly weak moments were in plugging the upcoming DVD release of the company's latest slapdash pandering. And give schlock some credit. It held my daughter's attention well enough that she scarcely noticed the waves of hawkers attempting to unload their trinkets, carefully timed to tie in with what was happening down on the ice.

By the middle of the second act, though, my daughter was asking when it would be over. What? She wanted it to *end?* Yes! Victory! It was a knockdown in the late rounds. No, not a knock-*out,* but it was enough to swing the judges' decision my way.

Disney, one; Captain Dad, one. I stood a chance to win the Mouse Wars yet.

The Spoils of Grandparenthood

So. We had this plan. My wife and I were *not* going to spoil our kids with too much *stuff*. The last thing I want is to deprive my children of meaningful hardship.

But we were first-time parents—to wit, clueless—and we had reckoned without grandparents. Particularly grandmas. Particularly grandmas with a first grandchild. Who's a baby girl.

Grandchildren are like a fantasy camp for women who have successfully passed motherhood. All the fun, none of the sleep deprivation. You can't blame them for going nuts. I knew that. But that didn't stop me from grumbling under my breath.

Then one day at work—you know, sitting in the playroom—I took a look around the room. First of all, you have to understand that our playroom is bigger than my first apartment. Literally. It was designed to be a formal living room but ended up as the island of misfit furniture once we moved in. In time, several items either found other rooms to call home or were given away. All that was left was a puffy sofa.

So when the baby came along, we turned it into a playroom.

There I was, then, with my now two-year-old, looking at the wall-to-wall rubber mat I had laid down over the floor, with it's colorful interlocking tiles, the letters of the alphabet, and our daughter's name around the perimeter; the plastic playhouse we bought her for Christmas as something to put in the corner but that could humanely shelter a Third World family; the pretend kitchen we got her because it was blue (Why not? It's *blue!* Her favorite color! Where else are we going to find one that's blue?);

"Mother, please! I can spoil my own child."

the tent, for roughing it outside the playhouse; the bookcase housing more volumes than any preschool library; the . . . the everything.

Everything *we* got her. Not her doting grammy.

We were the guilty ones! However innocently. And . . . well, at least I got a cartoon out of it. Though I probably used the proceeds to buy more toys.

CHAPTER 7

Testosterone Is for Wussies

So. Princesses, pretend kitchens, baby slings. Is this really my life? Seriously? Pockets full of baby wipes and diapers?

Is this the life of the former high school Catholic league state champ wrestler?[4] The life of the former rocket man? The former swaggering madman adman? What happened?

It did have me rethinking my masculinity, even before all those debilitating thwacks to the inseam. Then came that newspaper report that provoked primal roars from all the man caves on the Internet.

A team of scientists had discovered that men's testosterone levels decrease once they have children—and the more time they spend around their offspring, the steeper the decline. Yee gads! You'd think they'd changed NFL uniforms to tutus, there was such chest-thumping backlash among males of our species who took this as a direct challenge to their virility. Gruntingly they had defined themselves by their testosterone and thus they decried fatherhood as the end of manhood.

I freely confess that my own testosterone level corroborates this study. Why, it must have plummeted through the basement floor over these years of nonstop kid coddling, because this news got a rise out of not so much as my eyebrow. To the

....

4 Okay, it was the ninety-eight-pound weight class, but still . . .

knuckle draggers, this would imply I have no virility left to challenge.

Or . . . it could be that I had had the chance to think about this well in advance of the study. So I was prepared to interpret the findings differently. The way I see it, the loss of testosterone does not signify the end of manhood. It signifies the end of boyhood. To which I say a manly hurrah. Halelujah, even.

Testosterone is for wussies.

Gasp! How can I utter such gender treason? Well, since this was an allegedly scientific study, let's look at it the way men pride themselves in looking at things. Let's look at it scientifically.

Let's look, for example, at what testosterone really does to you and then ask, "Is that manly?"

Testosterone:

- makes guys jump out of the back of a moving pickup truck for no other reason than . . . well, for no reason.

- makes guys shout, "Boo-yah!" and think they've scored intellectual points in an argument for it.

- makes guys take steroids until their testicles retreat into their abdominal cavities just so they can do one thing or another with a ball (which of course "they" really can't do, because it's the drug, not them, doing it).

- makes guys want to go out with bimbos just so other guys can see them with the bimbos, but then turn around and smash a beer bottle against the head of any other guy who they catch actually looking at the bimbos.

- makes guys bet on anything, no matter how stupid. Like mortgage-backed securities. And then it makes them want to make more of the stupid things so other guys can bet on them. Even after they all realize that it is completely stupid, they refuse to stop, making more, more, more, until

> they've crashed the entire world economy. Then I don't know what makes them beg the government for a bailout or soothe their consciences with bonuses while blaming someone else for their testosterone-fuelled stupidity.

That's testosterone. ¿Es macho, o no es macho?

Look, I'm not saying testosterone can't be fun. But it does make guys do things one might fairly question the intelligence of. I mean, like butting heads. Literally. For fun. As in football, rugby, boxing, and boxing on ice, otherwise known as hockey. Football is the most common head-butt-fest in our culture. Whether it's in school or just a pickup game in a vacant lot, it's a rite of passage for America's male youth.

What guy doesn't remember lying flat on his back with stars spinning around his head and a feeling like he just tried to

French kiss a bullet train, only to have it all seem worthwhile the moment he hears, "Nice hit," wafting through his pudding-thick brain fog? And then he gets up, "shakes it off," and goes back for more. These are truly precious memories. They are our badges of honor.

But, alas, the other big not really news in the papers of late has been how this head butting literally scrambles guys' brains. Putting on our science hats again, how does all of this help the advancement of the species?

Luckily Nature, in Her great wisdom, saw fit to diminish our stupidity-inducing hormone once we came to the full flourish of manhood through fatherhood. (Actually it begins when you first fall in love.) You don't have to be Darwin to see the sense in that. Finding a mate is the brass ring. Emission accomplished. Testosterone can retire to the basement with your old Archie comics.

Seriously, if we held onto our full cup of testosterone, we dads would be saying things like, "Come on, don't be a chicken. Just cross the street. You can outrun that truck. You're three years old, for Pete's sake. Go! Go! Go—Oooooh! Boo-yah, that's gotta hurt."

Man—the species, not the dude—would have gone the way of the Neanderthal. But man, the dude, grew up. He became a man. With children of his own, he set aside childish things.

Testosterone is for boys the way coolness is for kids. Kids need to define themselves by something when they have yet to do anything significant with their lives. It's a placeholder for real achievement.

Like raising kids. Not just spawning them, raising them.

That's doing something with your life. That's why us guys who are actually doing it earn the title of Captain Dad.

What? You don't think raising kids is manly? Think you're even half the man your mom was? Then go ahead. Prove it. Try it for a day. A week. A year. Or six.

Or are you too much of a wussy? Bawk bawk bawk bawk!

Yeah, I thought so. Boo-yah.

CHAPTER 8

Wasting Time 101

By the time I get out of bed in the morning, I'm exhausted. All I really want to do is go back to bed. But kids are funny. They want to *do* something. Every day. So I have to find a way to fill the time between when I sleep and when they sleep. Ideally it should be an activity that won't wipe me out. And it should be one whose consequences I can live with, which means I can't just plop them in front of the ADHD-TV all the time, tempting as that may be.

All the experts tell you not to let kids watch TV before the age of two—and this started even before studies showed that Baby Einstein videos actually *stunted* cognitive development in children. We followed this dutifully for our first child, almost until she was three, in fact. But then we instituted a movie night, which soon metastasized into two movie nights a week, which eventually gave way to an additional dose of PBS Kids TV on Wednesday mornings. (We didn't choose PBS for the educational content, but for the absence of commercials designed to induce choruses of "I want that! And that! Oooh, can I have *that?*") Even this controlled dosage of video sedation, however, had the familiar, instantaneous effect of turning a child's jaw slack and arresting her eyes, causing them to be both focused and unfocused at the same time. I could easily see how kids become addicted. Parents, too.

I confess I've succumbed to it once or twice myself, if only to get the dishes done or make a phone call. Still, I try to resist, because I fear TV's ongoing influence, especially when my daughter starts singing, "I wanna be a rock star," in that constipated pop singer voice she must have learned while visiting someone with cable. My fear is rooted in the memory of a child my wife and I saw in a restaurant once. A family restaurant. In a globally recognized Family Fun Mecca. This four- or five-year-old girl (dressed like a seventeen-year-old going to a Spin the Bottle party) had been dining with her mother when she stood up from her table to dance to the fairly innocuous piped-in music. She grabbed her crotch and started pumping and thrusting and gyrating her hips to the beat, her tongue draped lustfully beneath deadened eyes. All I know is, she didn't learn that from Barney.

Luckily there are other things you can do until the beering hour or your kids are old enough for you to say, "Go outside and play." Which, these days, is not until college.

You can figure out for yourself the more obvious ideas, like turning on the hose or sprinkler for some summer fun. If you have a kid who dislikes hair washing, try sneaking one in by bringing the soap and shampoo out for a wacky wash down in the backyard. I did that with one of my girls and had the presence of mind to take pictures. The next time she whined in the tub about getting her hair wet, I showed them to her. We laughed, and we got in a few more fairly painless shampooings before she figured out the "but that was different" argument.

If you live in an area that has things like books or the Internet, then there is surely some sort of local guide that tells you all the obvious places to visit with kids. They're mostly paid venues, recommended by paying advertisers, but in a pinch you'll be happy to pay when you simply can't go another minute of providing 103 percent engagement with your children. So don't think I'm complaining.

In fact, those are probably all you need if you can remember this one rule: *Everything* is merely something to riff off of. Say you have the world's most perfect plan to take the kids to the world's most amazing children's museum, and it goes off the rails

BETTER PARENTING through DUCT TAPE

because you pass a pond with some ducks and your kids want to feed the lunch you packed for the museum adventure to the ducks, then that is not a plan gone bad. It is a plan gone horribly, horribly *right.* A twofer! You not only save the children's museum for another day, perhaps a rainy day when you desperately need a can't-miss diversion, but you'll have a fabulously spontaneous duck pond extravaganza that your kids will never stop talking about.

So. Plans are always, always, always starting points, not destinations. With that in mind, let's look at some of the less-expected ways to waste quality time with your kids.

Stroll, stroll, stroll. When your baby is little, it really doesn't matter what you do. I'm sure there is some child expert somewhere who will tell you that seeing different places is good for a child's cognitive development. So just start wandering. When your baby is very little and still taking two naps a day, when the first nap is over, stroll *to* lunch. Eat and feed the baby. Then stroll *home* from lunch, and—voila!—it's nap time again. Talk about low impact. Plus, you get the added benefit of a little exercise and mapping out where all the parks are in your neighborhood for when the baby gets a little older (and you can plop them in the baby swing and swing, swing, swing an easy half hour or more away).

Ride, ride, ride. We live in Chicago, which has an el train. Kids under seven ride free. So we occasionally hop aboard and just go. Downtown there are parking lots on the roofs of buildings. To a kid, that's wacky. There are tall buildings to marvel at.

Overheard on the Playground:

There are all kinds of strange people and strange smells to wonder about. Don't have a train? Ride a bus. What's more fun for a kid than schtoonking the schtoonker (or whatever you call that cord you pull that makes the *schtoonk* sound telling the bus driver you want the next stop)! Along the way, stop for a bite or to check out an old-fashioned ladies foundation garments store or a pawn shop or . . .

Posh, posh, posh. Have a downtown area nearby? Go explore the lobby of a big, fancy hotel. Act like you're out-of-town tourists who are staying there. Don't look like you're getting away with something—and you'll totally get away with it. Be sure to check out the ornate moldings and the artwork. And the restrooms! Seriously. It's an easy half hour and a perfect gap filler if you are waiting for some other main event to begin. Besides, if you're going to explore any area at all, especially with kids, you want to know where all the accessible restrooms are.

Not, not, not posh. Another great urban adventure is to explore alleys (in the country, backroads). This is an especially great way to kill time when your primary time waster came up a half hour short. And, let's face it, there is something cool about seeing the hidden side of town. You might even pick up some great home-improvement ideas. Or some pre-broken toys at a garage sale.

Signs, signs, everywhere are signs. Not just any signs, the really good ones. Like Thai restaurants and hair salons, which love to include puns in their names ("Beau Thai," "Curl Up & Dye"). For even more entertaining puns, check out the portable toilets ("Oui Oui," "LepreCAN"). And don't forget to seek out the simple signs that never meant to be entertaining. My local favorite is a humble convenience store named, "A-to-Z Things." Just don't ask for a 7-up. It begins with a number.

Drive, drive, drive. Drive through unfamiliar neighborhoods and visit playgrounds that you've never seen before. Even if the playground is a dud, the novelty will get you through a chunk of the morning.

Hike, hike, hike. No, I don't mean football. I mean finding a clump of trees somewhere to explore. If you live in a city or suburban area, you may have to drive a bit—but that gives you alleys and neighborhoods and signs on the way! And it doesn't have to be a national forest. It can be a forest preserve or simply some overgrown lots in an area that is not wall-to-wall developed. If you can't find woods, an open field or prairie or desert will do. If none of these are available, heck, wander into a pet store to look at some animals. Fish, birds, hamsters. Trust me, it's big fun.

Munch, munch, lunch. See chapter 9. Yes, it is worth its own chapter.

Play, play, play—with someone other than you. Sorry, you have to wait for this one to work really well. Until the kids are at least three or four, they pretty much only play *near* other kids. Not *with*. So the playdate is more of a "play" playdate. As in pretend playdate. That is, it's for the parents of the respective children to sit in the same room with another adult and talk about . . . something—anything—who cares! It's talking with another adult.

Once the children are of legitimate playdate age, wow. Someone *else* can be the attention provider for your kids. Someone their own age. When you get the inevitable, "Can you make a sound like a duck? Can you sound like a sheep? Can you sound like a cow?" you can answer, "No, but your friend can." And you can walk away from the playroom that now sounds like a barnyard and enjoy a moment's relative peace while you sweep up the crumbs that have been under the table since breakfast.

And it doesn't matter if you're dropping off your kids at someone else's house or they are dropping theirs off at yours. Once kids have someone else to play with, you're off the hook for a while. Seriously. It almost makes you want to have more kids of your own so there's a built-in playdate mate around the clock.

Almost.

Books, books, books. Let me put it like this: One. If nothing else, that's how many things I will be able to say that I've done right as a parent. One. All things considered, that's not a bad tally. Especially when you consider the degree of difficulty of that one thing.

I've managed to turn the phrase "Or else you won't get your book!" into an effective threat at bedtime. Splashing the mirror instead of brushing your teeth? "You want your book?" Stalling on the toilet as if you were someone . . . well, someone *my* age? "Get moving if you want your book." Not getting your jammies on? . . .

"Wow! Wouldn't it be cool to have this in pieces all over the floor?"

It's a great hammer. For you more "modern" parents who prefer affirmations, it works as a *positive* incentive, too. "Yay! You were great cleaning up the playroom. I'd say that deserves an extra book."

Or ten. Twenty. More! You can kill an entire afternoon with a good read-a-thon. If you time it right, you might even distract your kids enough to avoid that dreaded witching hour, where they are possessed by wild animal spirits each day. On a day when the weather is too rotten to go outside, or a kid is too sick to move, there is no greater keeper of the peace than a big stack of books.

"Are we going yet? . . . Are we going yet?"

As a bonus, this requires frequent trips to the library or bookstore. The children's section of each is bound to have the occasional read-a-thon of its own, with someone other than you doing the reading. It's amazing to watch someone in front of a room full of kids, speaking in a soft, nonthreatening voice and patiently displaying all the pictures for everyone to see. It makes you wonder, "Is this person clueless?" The kids start heckling and walking out.

A *professional* reader, on the other hand, uses a voice like a foghorn and only shows *that* there are pictures, but certainly doesn't slow down to dwell on them. The only thing with a shorter attention span than a child is a *group* of children. Remember: Mr. Rogers had cathode rays to hold children in their seats. A live reader has to radiate as much energy as a TV studio. But when you find a bookstore reader like that, you will brave the crowds she attracts to stalk her from bookstore to bookstore or library to library. Also hearing books read aloud in front of a test audience is a great way to shop for new additions.

Neat, neat, neat. Not as in "neato peachy keen!" but as in cleaning the playroom. Okay, it's not fun. The kids would rather eat their own heads than do it. They may even go so far as to tell you, "You're the meanest dad I ever had!" (You bet I wrote that one down.) So it takes a lot of yelling and threatening and headache. But it *does* eat up a lot of time.

And last, here is a tip that I simply cannot stress enough.

Never, never, never run errands! Call them *adventures*.

CHAPTER 9

Changing the World, One Diaper at a Time

I want to speak out on the age-old gender issue of potty parity. There is a scandalous inequity in our public restrooms. Can I get an amen?

Thank you, ladies. Except I'm not talking about the inequity you complain about at concerts and sporting events.

I'm talking about the unequal treatment of men in the world of child care. I'm talking about changing tables.

There are changing tables in every single ladies' room throughout the known universe. Men's rooms? Not so much. Okay, more than when I started this gig a few years ago, but still it's the exception, not the rule.

What accounts for such inequity? I hate to say such an ugly word, but the only one I can think of is *chauvinism.*

And an insidious form of chauvinism it is, too. Because it doesn't always meet your demographic biases.

I was in a too-hip-for-you restaurant in a waaaayyyy-too-hip-for-you neighborhood in Chicago, the sort of place where you dare not even recall that Lincoln was a Republican. It is down the block from the hippest baby store in the city (if you can believe the sign in the window), and it has an aggressively Progressive kid's menu. So if any place should be on the vanguard of modern parenting, you'd expect this place to be it. From my setup to this story, you have probably guessed by now that this restaurant does NOT have a changing table in the men's room. What is so funny about this? Well, I've been to the men's room at the docks in Skagway, Alaska, and there is a changing table there.

Docks in Skagway? Yes. Frou-frou kid-friendly hipster cafe in Wicker Park? No.

Whatever would I have done if I did not have a *woman* with me to change the diaper? In a pinch, I would have done what any Captain Dad would do. I'd improvise. If you want to hear about a guy's hidden creativity, ask him about the most difficult place he's ever had to change a diaper. "I remember being able to change a

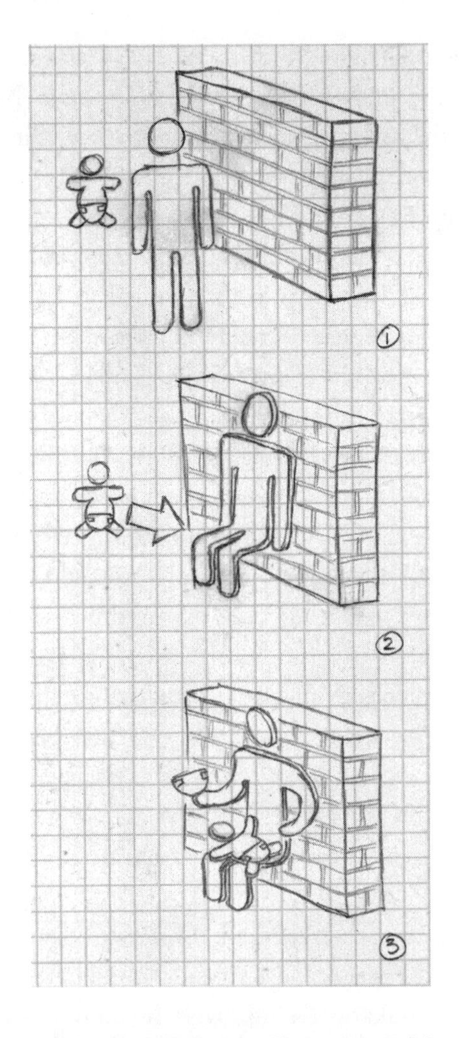

Captain Dad Portable Changing Table
(patent pending)

diaper," one friend has told me (no less than twenty times), "standing up in an airplane."

Depending on your circumstances, there are many ways to improvise a changing table. If you are still in the phase of carrying around a diaper bag, then you probably have a changing pad with you. The good news is that you can use the changing pad. The bad news is that you have no story to tell. Unless the change is necessary while you are driving, and the baby is wailing like crazy, so you have no choice but to pull over and lay the changing pad over the hood of your car. And it's rush hour. You get some story points for that. But in a men's room anywhere but a biker bar, not so much.

And then there are the places that are trying, but the architecture is old enough to be working against them. I'm talking about men's rooms that are too cramped for the retrofitted changing table, such that anything that accidentally falls off the table lands in a urinal. If you've ever changed a

fourteen-month-old with wildly kicking feet and loosely fitting shoes, you sort of wish the building had remained socially backward and let you improvise.

But here's the thing about the lack-of-changing-table parity. It's not men who should be outraged about it, but *women!*

More than three out of four married couples with young children consist of two working parents. This means they spend roughly the same number of hours with the kids. So when parents are out on the town with the kids, dads are there nearly as often as moms. Theoretically at least. And this means that when Nature calls in the middle of a family lunch at the family restaurant, the dad should be just as likely as the mom to attend to the matter. Theoretically at least. In a society that likes to imagine itself as progressive.

But!

Let's say the dad harbors certain atavistic tendencies about "women's work." But let's say that this dad is not so much of an atavist that he doesn't know not to mention these tendencies, lest he be branded as . . . well, as what he is. This dad can weasel out of diaper duty in a most insidious way. He can *volunteer* for it.

Then he simply has to disappear around the corner with the wee-soaked wee one, count to ten, then walk back to his wife, wearing a long face and grumbling, "Doggone it, honey, they don't have a changing table in the men's room. What kind of world is this anyway? But, hey. I can see you don't want to be bothered. So don't you worry your pretty little head. You just sit there and enjoy your lunch. There was a spot on the floor by the urinal, and it was

only a *little* wet. I could—" Boom. Done. He's off the hook. Even if he volunteers to lay some paper towels underneath the baby.

So, to my brothers in babes-in-arms who complain about there not being enough changing tables in men's rooms, I say: Guys, chill out. Brow-beating society into changing its ways to help you change a diaper is not your job. No, sir. That's *women's* work!

CAPTAIN DAD
Tot Tips

If you are a dad with small children, the stay-at-home type or not, then it goes without saying that whenever there is a mess to clean, you reach for whatever is handy. Typically that means baby wipes.

Wiping up spills? Toilet needs a wipe down? Pea puree on your sister-in-law's angora sweater? Baby wipes to the rescue. In fact, a dad's first response to any domestic equivalent of Hurricane Katrina is always baby wipes. I have personally washed the entire playroom floor with them. Why? Because they were there! What was I *supposed* to do, walk *all the way* to the kitchen or bathroom for a sponge and some cleanser? Puh-leeze.

How do our wives feel about this? Well, if you have to ask . . .

But! When my two-year-old did some extensive two-year-old journaling on the leather sofa with a ballpoint pen, my wife took the predictable paper towel and mild soap approach—with minimal results. Frustrated, she stepped away for a moment, only to return to a clean couch. And me with an ink-stained baby wipe in my hand. And a smug grin on my face.

Yes, baby wipes remove ink from leather sofas.

Baby wipes. They're not just for bottoms anymore.

CHAPTER 10

Let's Do Lunch

You could eat off the floor in my kitchen. In fact if you were willing to get down on your hands and knees, you could probably cobble together an entire meal. Of course, it would consist entirely of crumbs.

Yes, crumbs. Crumbs!

I spend a ridiculous amount of time sweeping up crumbs. Blizzards of them. It doesn't matter what the kids are eating—bananas!—there will be crumbs. Like sawdust at a mill, they fly with every buzz-cut nibble, no matter how many times I tell my kids to eat over their plates. If I used a rake instead of a broom, I could create my own Zen garden underneath the kitchen table.

So I sweep. After every meal. After every snack. After every time I just finished sweeping but somebody just *had* to come back for one more bite of something she hadn't quite finished. Like brunch after the Sermon on the Mount, you'd be astounded at the crumbous fallout one last little bite can rain upon your freshly swept floor—unless you have kids, that is. Then you know too painfully well.

A lazy man might suggest putting it off until the end of the day and sweeping them up all at once. I know, because I *was* that lazy man. And do you know what I found out? I found out that a *truly* lazy man will sweep early and often, because if he doesn't,

tiny little feet will ferry those crumbs to every corner of the house, like busy bees pollinating a grove of very flat polyurethaned trees. I can't tell you how many times I have found what I thought were maggots in the baby's room, only to be relieved to find it was only dried rice. Only to be *un*relieved at the subsequent thought of what other natural ant baits were hiding there.

So. Sweep. Learn to love it.

And I do. Sort of. I mean, sweeping does have a Zen-like appeal. It is a time I get to send the kids out of the room (shrieking, "Don't walk in my dirt!" just like my mother used to) and savor a moment's relative relief from my two little entropy machines. So long as I don't think about the chaos that is going on in the next room while I'm restoring order to the kitchen floor.

> Is it a sin to tell a lie even if it's to stop your kid from being such a messy eater? "You can't get married unless you've learned to eat neatly. That's why brides wear white, you know."

The Spork Brought Me

What I truly need is a moment's relative relief from these moments of relative relief. This is why, as often as possible, I like to eat lunch somewhere *other* than home.

It's a habit I developed in my single days. When you live alone and work at home, you need to do something to prevent you from turning into a pasty-faced troll slaving beneath a bare bulb dangling from a basement-ceiling joist. Similarly, when you stay home with kids all day, you need to get the heck out of the house to remind yourself that the world is still populated by people tall enough to appreciate the extent of your thinning hair. And recall the intellectual thrill of talking to a real live adult about something other than your kids. "Yes, make that a *large* drink."

Overheard on the Playground:

Best of all, you dramatically increase your odds of sitting through an entire meal without having to get up for another glass of milk, or a different spoon, or a paper towel to mop up a spill, or no I wanted my apple with the skin off, no, *on! ON!* **ON!** dang it's too late and I'm not going to cut up another apple just because you can't make up your mind and I still haven't had a chance to sit down and oh for crying out loud can't you eat over your plate it looks like Hansel and Gretel spent the last week wandering lost beneath your chair and—

Somebody else will sweep up the crumbs.

The only problem is, you can't go to all the places you used to before kids. Okay, maybe at first, when your baby is still on an exclusive diet of milk or formula. Or maybe even when she advances to that mushy stuff people have the gall to call "solid food." But when she's old enough for human food, you need to find a place that is Kid Friendly.

Lots of restaurants like to call themselves Kid Friendly, but it's only to pad their key words in an Internet search. To them all

it means is having a high chair or two. But don't be fooled. Truly Kid Friendly means a whole lot more.

First, it means you can pay for your meal up front. Young children are volatile and can suddenly boil over, shrieking like a tea kettle, leaving you no option but to scoop them up and bolt for the door. It's tacky to do that before paying the check. And if you have to wait, you *will* wait, watching the waitress taking her sweet old time because she knows that every second of humiliation you suffer because of your wailing child means another dollar of guilt tax you will feel obligated to add to her tip.

When kids are just a little bit older, you need that flexibility for other reasons. To keep misbehavior to a minimum, you need to be able to make good on the threat of, "One more time, and we are going home. I don't care if you haven't finished your sandwich." Again, if you have a waiter who is not lightning personified, you're fried.

Kid Friendly also means loud, but not too loud. You want enough noise to cover you in case all conversation stops the very instant your little dumpling blurts, "Do you think anyone else here is wearing Thomas underpants?" I mean, you certainly don't want to be in a staid downtown club when that happens. Trust me.

But you don't want it to be Chuck E. Cheese loud either. You'll get enough chances to take ibuprofen as a parent without that headache. Similarly you don't want a place to be a total dive, but neither do you want it so nice that you sweat the "Wreck of the Hesperus" being reenacted underneath your table.

Napkins. I know this is an obvious one, but a kid-friendly joint has to have abundant napkins. If a restaurant wanted to add a napkin surcharge for people with small children, I'd pay it without question. But the last thing you want is a place that is stingy about the napkins. Even if they do have six tasty subs with less than six grams of fat.

Spoons are also nice. Not every place with plastic tableware has them. Forks will usually get you by, but spoons are often so much better with young people who have yet to finish finishing school. Or learned not to eat with their hands all the time.

The gold standard of Kid Friendliness, however, is sporks.

What is it about a spork that cries, "We understand kids!" so clearly? They're fun, they're practical, they have a delightful name that can give a five-year-old a topic of conversation that lasts an entire meal. If I ever establish a Captain Dad restaurant review, I won't give stars as my rating, I'll give sporks.

And now we come to that thing called the Kids' Menu. What is on it varies from restaurant to restaurant. (Two, three, four . . .) Okay, that was a joke for the parents who eat out with their kids. I'll take a moment for you to stop laughing . . . Still waiting . . . Still waiting. . . . While I'm waiting, let me explain the joke to those of you who don't eat out a lot with your kids. A kids' menu *never varies.* Whether you are at the Kebab Hut or the Sushi Hole or the Burger Bin, it's exactly the same: grilled cheese, chicken nuggets, mac 'n cheese, and hamburger. For lunch, add a PB&J. Some gussie it up, like doing the grilled cheese as a quesadilla or cheese pizza (i.e., grilled cheese with ketchup). Maybe even breaded cheese sticks. Or calling chicken nuggets "dino" nuggets or chicken "tenders."

I've heard tales of restaurants that serve more exotic items on the kids' menu. Like fish and chips. But what is the "fish" but a batter-fried nuggety substance that parents will tell their kids tastes like chicken? So, quibbling semantics aside, a kids' menu is a kids' menu is a kids' menu.

For a drink, it's 2 percent milk or a juice box. How hard would it be to serve skim? Or even 1 percent? Or hasn't anybody read about the scourge of childhood obesity these days?

On the other hand, there's juice. I remember the first time we gave our daughter juice. We went for a stroll one day after church and stopped in a Jamba Juice for a grown-up treat. We watched all those healthy fruits go into the blender and didn't think anything of allowing our new solid-food eater a taste, if only to expand her horizons beyond milk and Cheerios.

Until she started snarling and spinning like the Tasmanian Devil, demanding more, *more, MORE!* What had gotten into her, we wondered? Ah. The light went on. We had just given her *juice.* Duh. It's pure sugar. Or, to your doctor, pure poison.

Maybe you scoff. *Pure* sugar, you ask? *Pure* poison? Okay, you got me. It's not pure at all. You're too smart for me. Obviously you read that newspaper article that reported that 10 percent of apple and grape juice samples tested in a lab had been found to contain more than the government sanctioned "safe" levels of . . . wait for it . . . arsenic.

Arsenic? Wait, I thought. *Aren't apple seeds rumored to have arsenic? And maybe the same is true with grape seeds. So maybe this arsenic is natural and safe.* Until I looked it up and learned that it was *cyanide* that's in apple seeds. As for grape seeds, I have no idea.

Overheard on a Playground in a Neighborhood Much More Upscale Than Our Own:
"Sushi! Sushi! Sushi for lunch!"

So if it isn't the seeds, the arsenic must simply be an additive. In which case, why isn't it listed in the ingredients? Unless it's simply ambient arsenic. And, to be fair, who doesn't have a few bowls of arsenic potpourri scattered around the house or factory?

Now, if arsenic can simply float its way into your kid's juice, doesn't it kind of make you wonder, what *else* is in there?

Why, lead, of course. Yep, another spot-checking of juice boxes—juice *boxes,* as in, for kids—in California found a whopping 85 percent of them with lead levels above the legal limit for tap water.

Anyway, despite the formidable sugar, fat, arsenic, and lead content in kids' menus, some parents (alas, I am one of them) desperately crave one meal a day where they don't have to spend an extra half hour cleaning up afterward. And they get to sit and eat without getting up every two seconds to refill a glass or get something different because a picky eater changes his or her mind after the first bite.

So here's my crazy million-dollar idea. What if—brace yourself, it's really crazy—what if someone developed a kids' menu that offered kids something *remotely* healthy *and* yummy at the same time? The kids' parents would actually *want* to come back. And come back *often*. Repeat business is gold for restaurants! Why wouldn't someone want to encourage it?

Unless they really *don't* want the place overrun with kids, which I can sincerely understand. But if they don't want kids, why even pretend? Why not put Leek Surprise and Cauliflower Clots on the kids' menu? Or have no kids' menu at all?

I'm not just ranting, I'm offering a gold mine for some plucky young entrepreneur out there. Start a restaurant with a yummy You-Can-Eat-Here-Every-Day-and-Still-Avoid-Childhood-Obesity kids' menu, and not only will you get Captain Dad's Five Spork rating, you'll also find yourself on the cover of *Forbes* in the first six months.

Even if you don't have sporks.

That Thing That You Do

I remember sitting at lunch with my older daughter and feeling her little foot pressed against my knee like it was a footrest. She did it for years. It could be annoying at times, but I didn't say anything because there was something impossibly sweet about it, and I knew I'd miss it when she got bigger. She's not only bigger now, she's also in school all day. No longer my constant lunch companion.

Her little sister and I now go off to eat on our own. I was thinking about this the other day—when I felt another little foot using my knee as a footrest.

I didn't say anything.

CHAPTER 11

Smackdown in Orlando

I was on my way to a vacation, which is sort of a misnomer. When you are the full-time parent, a vacation with the kids is anything but a vacation. And when you are the full-time parent *and* the dad, it's even worse. Not only are you the go-to parent while on "vacation," but you are also the sherpa. You are not only "always on," everything is always on *you*. Every problem, every errand, every piece of equipment and clothing. And at least one kid.

Anyway, we were going to . . . (*dramatic musical sting*) . . . Disney World.

Now if you didn't just crack open the book here, you will know that I embarked on this journey with more than a little trepidation. And you can probably suspect who engineered it (hint: the Queen Mother). I may have survived the bout with *Disney on Ice* and the ninety-eighth consecutive viewing of *The Little Mermaid,* but descending into the lair of my enemy for three terror-filled days had me questioning my decision to become a parent in the first place. Resentment wafted from my pores, but there was no sense in wasting energy trying to resist. I was going to Disney World.

The grudge match was on.

We decided not to tell then-four-and-a-half-year-old Rebecca where we were going—or even that we were going

> **Captain Dad Tot Tip:**
> The tray tables on an airplane are strong enough to hold at least a twenty-eight-pound toddler (or more, but I haven't tested it yet). Now who says that you can't find a changing table on an airplane!

anywhere at all—until we got to the airport. Grammy lives near the airport, and we had shipped off Rebecca to stay with her the night before we left. So far, nothing seemed unusual. Then Grammy took her to "watch the planes." Give the woman credit. The ruse worked. In fact Rebecca is so happy to do anything whatsoever with her grandmother that she completely ignored the fact that they had brought luggage with them and that her parents also showed up from clear across town to "watch the planes." Also with luggage. We had withheld mention of the grand adventure because we knew Rebecca would not sleep between the time she knew and the time she actually set foot on Hallowed Ground. Even telling her there in the airport, we feared the sheer excitement of it would cause her to vibrate into another dimension.

We asked her to guess where we were going. She guessed it was to visit relatives in Oregon. We told her it was Disney World. She cried, "But I want to go to Oregon!" A hopeful beginning, from my point of view.

But it finally sank in when she saw the actual words, Orlando, FL, above the flight gate. She grew eerily serene. A glowing orb of contented child flesh. The sight of her hypnotized even me into a temporary serenity.

But once we touched the ground, my inner cynic emerged. You wouldn't have noticed it, though, because I was buried under bags and strollers and all the requisite bivouac paraphernalia of the modern parent. You see, we had brought along our one-and-a-half-year-old Lucy as well.

Traveling with young children is like riding herd on a monkey drive. I was grumbling by the time I wrangled our mountain of gear into the trunk of a cab. And we hadn't yet addressed the matter of rustling our kids inside. Rebecca wouldn't be a problem. Heck, we could probably have tethered her to the antenna, and she would have floated behind in the breeze, she was so buoyant by that point; but Lucy had to be strapped in like a normal human child.

We had arranged the cab ahead of time, so the driver had been forewarned to have child safety seats in the backseat of his vehicle. But they had been tossed in there loosely. He had no idea how to buckle them in. He had never done it before. "I never had children of my own," he explained with a shrug. I looked up at him, an affable man in his fifties.

And my heart broke.

Perhaps you noticed that I am not the most sentimental guy on the block. But my heart ached for this man—physically—even as I had been lamenting my own twisted fate. Even amid the chaos and aggravation of traveling with small children. This poor man would never know such suffering: He had "never had children."

I felt a rush of gratitude for my "suffering." I felt blessed by it.

This, I feared, was a bad omen for my keenly cultivated grudge. Was there perhaps a chink in my Disney-repellent armor? Okay, enough foreshadowing. On with the story.

The plan was to settle into our Disneyfied hotel, get to bed early, then assault the gates at the crack of dawn. Get in, get on six or seven rides before the park knows what hit them. And, sure enough, we hit that many rides in the first ninety minutes, more than most latecomers manage in a whole day. But getting there before the crowds doesn't mean that you can get there before the Disney Army sees you coming. Oh, no. They're there lying in wait. Bright-eyed funsters are posted outside the gate to get you

emotionally programmed to love every wallet-sucking minute. And who is first in their sights? The kids?

No way. It's the dads.

Dads carry the wallet, after all. So the funsters gotta loosen 'em up. Line 'em up, get 'em to do the Hokey Pokey. Let 'em see the kids laughing at what a great guy Dad is, so easygoing, so willing to go along. Let 'em know that they are not in charge. Mickey is.

I rolled my eyes at this charade and thought, *So far, so good;* cynicism intact. I even discovered a cynical admiration for the place. From the lip-synched park-opening ceremony hosted by the "mayor," to the smartly placed gauntlet of gift shops that they had the gall to name Main Street USA, seemingly blind to the irony of what corporatized retailing has done to the real Main Street, USA.

And then there was the slogan, "The Most Magical Place on Earth," which has at least one obvious interpretation: They can make a year of private education disappear in three days.

No joke. The cost for a three-day trip was more than a year's private school tuition for our children.

But give Disney this: They do make paying for things about as easy as possible. They'll happily accept cash, credit, or healthy organs. On the jungle boat ride, even *they* joke about their efficiency in separating you from your cash at every bend. The only opportunity they seemed to overlook was that there was no valet parking for strollers at each of the rides. Note to Disney management: big money-making possibility lost here (P.S. I want a cut of the dough. I've got schools to pay for).

"What'll it be girls? Private schools or *Disney On Ice*?"

As for the food, well, it isn't the Ritz. The Ritz is cheaper (*ba dump bump*). When they hand you your receipt, you don't think of it as a receipt so much as evidence of the incredible claim that you could, in actual fact, pay nine dollars and five cents for a tiny bag of popcorn and a Diet Coke.[5] Now, I know what you're thinking. I'm a cartoonist married to a public servant. If anybody's flush in this economy, it's us. And, yeah, I suppose, in the big scheme of things, I can spare the $9.05USD for my popcorn and

....

5 Actual example.

a European-size Diet Coke, but that's not the point. The point is that the woman at the cash register gave me a smile like she knew she had gotten away with something. Like one of those bankers with the federal bailout money. So my gripe is not about the money so much as the idea of it.

And, of course, there's the money.

I'm not saying that this place is too expensive for a family with two working parents, but I am *suggesting* that it is a major reason why so many families *need* two working parents.

But surely I was able to justify all this cost better once I saw all the attractions. There was the famous Space Mountain (sorry, too scary for little kids), the Pirates of the Caribbean (too scary for *my* kids), and the Haunted Mansion (just the name . . .). But they also had a life-size replica of the Swiss Family Robinson's tree house. And here we found my daughters' absolute favorite attraction of all. Not the tree house, but the cool-down station just outside of it. Giant tiki heads spraying a fine mist. What could be more thrilling? We seriously couldn't pull them away. I could have been riding roller coasters,

Captain Dad Tot Tip:
Rent a car or take a taxi to the nearest non-Disney grocery store and stock up on snacks, breakfast, and lunch food. Buy a nice little backpack while you're at it to carry your food with you to whichever kingdom you visit (yes, even Epcot). The savings will not only pay for your cab or car rental and then some, but you will actually enjoy your meals.

and here I was with an oversize, spitting mask. Was I doomed to three days of *this?*

No, of course not. There was greater absurdity in store: costume chasers.

One of the things that amused me when I first arrived were the parents following their kids from costumed character to costumed character, standing in ridiculously long lines, just to get autographs. Mary Poppins, Tigger, Alice (of Wonderland fame). And some strange bear whom I'd never seen in a cartoon but seemed to be some sort of official Disney mascot known only to the people who worked there. These weren't the *real* characters, of course. They were low-paid actors working mainly for experience. They had had to learn to forge the signatures of their respective characters, which were designed by graphic artists in a studio somewhere across the continent.

How I pitied those parents, dunned into such a vain pursuit. And how much more I pitied them an hour or two later—when I became one of them. Official Disney autograph book and Mickey pen in hand, my Rebecca was in absolute heaven. She got to see real, live Princesses. And *we* got to stand for hours in a surreal sort of receiving line. Inch by inch, we slogged toward our personal audience with the Princesses, pulling every trick imaginable to maintain our and our children's composure along the way, finally getting to the very front of the line in time to hear our own little princess squeal, "I have to use the bathroom—*really bad!*" God bless our fellow long-suffering parents who allowed us to bolt the line without losing our place.

Then, just when we had survived the Princesses ordeal, we had to get into an *even longer line* to meet the Fairies. But not *all* the Fairies. It was Silvermist's day off. Silvermist is the one who wears blue, which means we would have to come back. Blue is Rebecca's favorite color. Therefore Silvermist is her favorite fairy.

My wife and I had a strategy session before we returned that next day. Like our early onslaught to the park, we figured that the line might be shorter if we ran to the court of the Princesses and Fairies the very moment that section of the park opened, which was about an hour after the Magic Kingdom as a whole opened. Except we weren't the only ones to have figured that out. We all stood there at the Toon Town gate with a horde of other park gamers, waiting . . . waiting . . . until the gates opened and everyone took off like a—well, running was against park rules. So picture a speed-walking version of the running of the bulls in Pamplona.

Somehow, though, we managed to fit in some rides. Peter Pan, Winnie the Pooh, and It's a Small World particularly. Okay, almost exclusively. Winnie was a huge hit with our younger daughter Lucy. It occurred to me on about the one hundredth ride that she looks a lot like a little Pooh-bear herself. I took her picture by a big Pooh cutout because they looked so cute together.

That's when it occurred to me that the place was starting to get to me. I had to seek out ways to keep up my cynicism. Like noticing the way a determined four-and-a-half-year-old could break the steering column in one of the cars in a Tomorrowland ride because she let the car slam so hard and so repeatedly into the guide rail (note to Disney lawyers: I'm not admitting anything here; it's pure conjecture—about someone else's kid). Or how a calypso band was ringing out a sprightly steel drum version of what most people know as the *M*A*S*H* theme, but which happens to be

Captain Dad Tot Tip:
If you miss the crack-of-dawn ride siege, you can also beat the lines in the evening when everyone is watching the parade. But only if you go for multiple days, because you'll have to see the parade at least once to see Real Live Disney Characters!

a song entitled "Suicide Is Painless." No wonder the musicians were smirking like that.

What was admirable about the park, however, was that in three long days at the parks, among tens of thousands of families from all walks of life, I only saw one parent slapping a child. It was at the end of a day. And perhaps this is another reason they switched from the Happiest to the Most Magical Place on Earth, because it is indeed magical that among so many overexhausted, overstimulated children—with their even more overexhausted, overstimulated parents—this was the only violent conflagration; and it rang more of extreme exasperation than habitual abuse. So that's definitely a positive thing. Unless, of course, it's simply because Disney saps the parents of the energy to swat anyone anymore, which would fall into the plus column as well.

Thus, with great effort, I fancied that I was battling Disney to a draw in the Smackdown in Orlando as we headed into the final round.

But I had forgotten about what happened after a special event on our first night there. We attended a special after-hours trick-or-treating party (the entire month of October is Halloween at Disney World!). When we got back to our room that night, before collapsing in bed, Rebecca gushed how she had met Minnie Mouse—for the second time already in one day—and had her picture taken with her, also for the second time. She jabbered happily about Minnie as she sorted her trick-or-treats. She put all her favorite treats in one bag. Fairly typical for a kid her age. But—(*ominous music*)—she had an *atypical* plan for that bag.

By Day Three, we were all dragging, no one more so than Rebecca. That kid expends as much energy as the Main Street Electrical Parade on an ordinary day's excitement at home. Here, at her own most magical place in the world (outside of Grammy's house), the terawattage her little body generated could have eliminated our dependency on foreign oil. But it was the third day, and her internal dynamo's bearings were shot. She took a long nap that afternoon and woke up with a fever. We should have stayed in the hotel and rested before our trip home the next day. But nothing could deter her from returning to the Magic Kingdom for one last visit before our pilgrimage came to an end.

Sick and weary, she boarded the shuttle (the only free thing at Disney, incidentally), clutching her candy bag protectively against her chest. She could barely be persuaded to go on her favorite ride (Peter Pan) one more time before she homed in on her target. We stood in line with our wilting little flower of a child. She draped herself over the ropes as boneless as the old-fashioned cartoon characters who danced on the screen over our heads to distract us as we waited for one last audience with the First Couple. Poor Rebecca. Limp. Played out. Could this be a repeat of *Disney on Ice*? Would I eke out another judge's decision in the Smackdown in Orlando?

The moment came when we were ushered in to the anteroom to freshen up before being presented to Mickey and Minnie. Rebecca came alive, animated by some hidden reserve of internal grace. When ushered into the innermost sanctum, she stepped forward with her bag of favorite candies—not the candies she did not like, but *all* her favorites—and chimed with a silver-toned sweetness, "Here, Minnie. I brought these for you."

The actress in the big-head outfit was no doubt a talented one, but never talented enough to react with such spontaneous knee-buckling emotion. After endless hours of daily grip-and-grin photo ops with the kiddies, she was clearly and genuinely touched.

But not me. I was flat on my back. Knocked out. By a mouse in a polka-dotted jumper who could inspire such selflessness in a little girl. And by the little girl herself, of course.

Sure, I lost the Smackdown. But I was not ashamed. Hell, I was proud to be knocked out that way. Who wouldn't be? Because, that sweet little girl? I'm her dad.

Ten Toy Labels I Fully Expect to See

In advertising, these kinds of labels are called "violators." And now you know why.

CHAPTER 12

Green Parenting

When our older daughter was born, we were typical middle-aged hypervigilant first-time parents. We changed her at the first misting or smudge, which means we were burning through diapers at a rate of nearly twenty a day.

I'm not kidding. It was on her birth announcement:

Length: 20 inches

Weight: 7 pounds 3 ounces

Diapers per day: 19

We regretted that little bit of too much information almost immediately though. We live in an environmentally conscious enclave. Our neighbors are big boosters of tolerance too, thankfully, so they chuckled dutifully about this little nineteen-diapers-a-day "joke." But we got the message. We needed to ponder our carbon buttprint.

In a fit of eco-conscience, we marched right out and bought a case of biodegradable diapers. Thus proclaiming to the world, "We are green parents!"

By "green," of course, I mean "hopelessly naive." Because if you have ever bought biodegradable diapers, it is a sure bet that you only did it once and swore never again. It's not the brown-paper-bag aesthetic that made these an unviable choice. It's the fact that they didn't work. Sorry, Gaia, but they really didn't.

They freaking leaked. We ended up throwing out most of the box (very environmentally unfriendly), running several unanticipated loads of laundry (also eco-bad), and casting aspersions at the planet in the heat of the moment (as if the planet needs more heat).

So in a refit of our ecoconscience, we slunk right out and bought a case of Huggies. Thus ended our period of Green Parenting. But maybe you'll have better luck today. Years have passed, and maybe biodegradable diaper technology has evolved, despite the fact that technological evolution is not exactly the *raison d'être* among biodegradable diaper proponents.

Still, it's not like the Captain Dad household doesn't do what it can for Mother Nature. For instance, my children are always picking up garbage. Until I slap it out of their hands and yell at them for the millionth time not to pick up garbage off the ground. But sometimes it actually makes it into trash cans. And, either way, for a moment it is not defiling the earth. So that's something.

We also conserve water. Of course we do it by not washing our children's hair as often as prescribed. This has the added benefit of reducing noise pollution, what with all the screaming that seems to be part of the hair-washing process. These efforts do not go unnoticed either. People love to observe how green our children are. But don't worry, it's just mold. A little bleach and a wire brush, and it comes right off.

We protect the planet in other ways, too. We practice the middle-class Caucasian enviro-friendly custom of using so much sunscreen that our children's skin reflects the sun's warming rays back into space. Seriously, go to a park these days, with all those zinc-oxided faces; it's like Marcel Marceau Day Camp. Only noisier.

And let's not forget the times I curbed my personal CO_2 emissions by not exhaling. Such as when my three-year-old insisted on scaling a climbing wall all by herself. Or took a nap without a pull-up for the first time. Oh, yes. I held in those greenhouse gases until they dissolved back into my blood.

The kids do their share to fight greenhouse gases, too. Avoiding vegetables decreases their methane emissions.

And they are boffo at not overburdening the nation's landfills with unwanted plastic toys. No, sirree. Every toy, no matter how

battered, raggedy, broken, or unplayed with for years, is too precious to be thrown away. In the end, their buckets-of-tears pleas always sway me to preserve these national treasures by simply stowing them away in the attic—where they serve as insulation! An ecological perfecta.

Hand-me-down clothes are a classic Green Parenting practice, and we were prepared to sustain this practice even if our second child was not another girl. Our first daughter's favorite color was blue. So what if some of the skirts were a little frilly? Call it a kilt. Besides, half her undies for a while were traditional Y-fronts with Thomas the Tank Engine and Cars prints. We would have gotten her proper girl's panties, but, for some sexist reason, the underwear makers refuse to make girl's underwear with those characters despite the fact that girls seem to enjoy them almost as much as boys.

Green Parenting also gives you something to do with all those Christmas and birthday presents labeled "1,001 Sharp Pieces!" or

"Now LOUDER and More AnNoYiNg!" or "Glitter! Glitter! Glitter!" Instead of feeling guilty regifting such atrocities, think of it as doing your share for a sustainable future. We sure do.

On a related note, I am working on a numbering system for the toy manufacturers to use to help people recycle toys more efficiently. It's like the recycling code you find on plastics. For instance, a #1 might be something benign that you could give your sister's child and still preserve familial relations, whereas a #6 would be a toxic splatter of pointy chards that you dump on that overly solicitous neighbor who calls your child by her middle name because she thinks that's what you really should have named her and always remembers birthdays with ideological gifts that border on creepy, like stuffed animals that spout affirmations.[6] As soon as I find the right government agency to implement this code, I'm sure you'll find it extremely useful.

Meanwhile, green toys do exist. They are fairly easy to spot because they are made of wood. Wood! Or cloth. Cloth made of sustainable or recycled fibers. Wood or cloth. Those are your choices. Period. These toys have an almost magical effect on children. When all they get are wood and cloth toys, they miraculously stop begging for more. That's how fun these toys are! And what makes them so sustainable.

Okay, seriously. I do care about the environment and hope to instill similar values in my children, but not to the point that they call themselves, as some eco-enthusiasts do, "greenies." When I

....

6 Based on an actual gift but fictionalized enough so that no actual person says, "Hey, that's me!"

was a kid that meant "boogers." My guess is that, in kid circles, it still does. And environmentalists wonder why they have trouble appealing to the broader public.

One green initiative I actively support is buying organic milk, even at those much higher prices. This is because, while my Y chromosome endows me with a healthy appreciation of breasts, I am not so keen on seeing them on a third grader. So I try to limit the amount of bovine growth hormone I give my girls. I'd like to see them get all their permanent teeth before they get their permanent boy magnets. Heck, if they remain flat chested until after their wisdom teeth come in, that's just fine with me. It gives me a few more years before I have to invest in a shotgun.

And I wasn't just kidding about conserving water. I'm all in favor of it. Especially when it saves me work. Like with a dishwasher. Believe it or not, it's greener than old-fashioned hand washing, because it consumes way less water. Feeling very green about that, I tried to one-up my greenness with an "environmentally safe" dishwashing detergent. Okay, to be honest, the real reason I tried it was to escape the Citrus Fresh Scent or Mountain Pine Breeze Scent or Calypso Surfactant Mist Scent that pollutes all conventional dishwashing soaps.

Really? Explain to me the logic of adding a fragrance to your plates. Call me a fussy eater, but I do not want a whiff of pine with my spaghetti. The only dishwasher soap that is fragrance free is the eco-greenie soap. Except it isn't as eco-chummy as it purports to be, because . . . (you can see this coming, can't you?) just like the diapers, it doesn't work that well. I'm okay with wasting water to rinse dishes before putting them in the dishwasher, but having to wash them thoroughly before *and* after just doesn't strike me as true-blue green. So if you're in the conventional dishwashing detergent business, might I recommend a hot new flavor—all-new Simply No Scent?

As for other cleaning products, I used to be a fan of harsh chemical cleansers—the harsher the better!—but that was during my bachelor days, when my time between cleanings required the Augean Stables treatment. Now that I have to clean more responsibly, I want to clean . . . well, more responsibly. At first I thought that killing off all the bacteria and other microscopic bugs was the responsible way. And it's easy to do, because everything these days advertises its antibacterial power, even those back-to-school pencils (no joke; I guess they figure it's appealing to parents because you know your kid will be chewing on them). But it turns out that eradicating all the microbugs in your home is kind of like eradicating all the weights and treadmills in a gym. Kids' immune systems actually need these training germs to spar with. These bantamweight bouts strengthen them for the heavyweight title bouts we all face sooner or later. Oh, and there's that thing about the cleansers killing off all the helpful bacteria our bodies need too, but who really likes to think about the fact that somewhere between three and six pounds of our bodies is made of happy little parasites that our bodies need to survive? Ew. Yes, I say that even as a member of the snips and snails and puppy dogs' tails gender. Ew.

But remember that old adage about kids needing to eat a bushel of dirt by the time they turn five? Somewhere inside their sterile laboratories, scientists are churning out more and more support for that idea. Asthma and food allergies particularly have been linked to germless home environments and overwashing of everything.

Uh-oh. I feel another inspiration coming on.

"Introducing new Bushel O' Dirt Chewable Daily Supplements!" Yes! This one will not only make me rich, it will make me *filthy* rich. Which is just what the doctor ordered.

And if that isn't "Green Parenting," I don't know what is. Move over, Al Gore. Make way for Captain Dad!

Now where's my Nobel Prize?

FILTH

We all know the acronym MILF. It's tacky, to be sure (if you don't know what it means, then you can Google it, because I wouldn't dare spell it out in a G-rated book). Still, there is an element of flattery in it. Moms can be beautiful. Desirable.

So where is the male equivalent? If guys who stay home with the kids are half as sexy as the women pundits would have you believe, where is our acronym? How come you never hear about a FILTH? That is, Father I'd Like to Hug.

Hmm, wait. Maybe that's it. Maybe we need a better acronym.

CHAPTER 13

Talk Dirty (Diapers) to Me, Baby

In our callow youth we fantasize about what marriage will be like. Our daydreams are a stew of fairy tale extracts and spicy couplets from Byron, Blake, and Shelley, which we were forced to read in school. Maybe a snippet of sophisticated conversation from an old film where no one is ever without a martini.

We never imagine the actual words our mortal beloveds will one day whisper over the phone on their commute home from work: "Did she poop today? What was it like?" Nor do we imagine how blithely we will reply, "Mushy. I'm trying to get more water into her." (FYI, whether the poo is a mushy blob or hard little poo balls, the answer is always more water. Why? How the hell would I know? Just give the kid more water.)

You see, the romantic poets never allude, even cryptically, to the little poopsters who, it turns out, are the natural consequences of requited love. Maybe because, once their garrets were filled with the thudding thunder of little feet, they had neither the time nor the peace to write anymore. Fairy tale writers similarly punted on the issue with a glib "happily ever after" (which happens to be an anagram for "appear ever filthy," so perhaps they actually were sending us a secret message).

Now here comes the *really* disturbing part. When you offer an engaged response to your wife's scatological inquiries, she will *love* you for it. No, seriously! Is that amazing or what? After all the times she rolled her eyes at your fart jokes!

But, as they say, kids change everything. When you are married and take an interest in your *kids'* poops, you come across as sensitive. Sensitive! Ha! How come you never see *that* tip on the cover of *Cosmo*? "46 Sexy Ways to Describe a Diaper Blowout. Try Them Tonight!"

I'm not suggesting overdoing it. As with all things, there is such a thing as going too far. I mean, just because diapers have been an all-consuming part of my life for more years than I spent at college doesn't mean you'll be seeing me wear a Huggies sweatshirt into a sports bar. College, by contrast, is something people tend to get nostalgic about.

> **Captain Dad Tot Tip:**
> Busy little hands. Infants have busy little hands. Grabby little hands. So you should always do your best to keep them busy with something to grab—toys, books, dirty socks, sharp objects—anything—when changing a poopy diaper. Or guess what they will grab. You have been warned.

Four Years of College for *This?*

Thus it is that I seldom revisit the memory of a certain experience. Well, calling it a memory may be a bit of an overstatement; sleep deprivation and my attempts to repress the memory may have blurred things somewhat; so forgive me if some of the details are not the way you remember it. Yes, yes of course, I do remember that you weren't there; my point is that you can almost certainly recall the very same story from your own experience—unless you're better than I am at memory repression.

I vaguely recall one of my daughters (lucky for them I cannot remember which—or at least that's my story and I'm sticking to it) when she was barely toddling—probably about a year and some months old. Anyway, even at that age kids need periodic bathing. When they start to smell like a pet shop, you know it's time to pop them into the tub and hope they get a little water on them. The trick sometimes is finding the time to do it.

Survival in a home with very small children depends on a schedule. First, you live under the tyranny of nap time and bedtime. Get too lax with those, and your child will never get into any of the Really Good Schools. Then there is the allowance for pre-bedtime and pre-nap time rituals, which can grow to rival the time and formality of a Japanese tea ceremony if you're not careful. Then there are meals plus the time set aside for Mommy when she gets home from work. Working dads *like* to spend time with their children. Working moms *need* it. I'm sorry if that sounds sexist, but that's the way it appears to this casual observer. Regardless, *my wife* needs it. So I have always bent over sideways (which is way harder than backward if you ever tried it) to accommodate her. Which means I would have to be flexible with other, less important things in the schedule—such as bath time.

Overheard on the Playground:

Because, as you probably know, multiple conflicts can arise in any day's schedule. One parent may be held up at work, meaning she is coming home late for dinner; or maybe one knows that he simply won't have the energy to administer a bath if he waits until the very end of the day. So he opts for a morning bath while Mommy is gone, and he not only succeeds in getting the bath out of the way, but he also avoids having to think of something more creative to do with a morning, such as pretending that the Play-Doh was confiscated in a midnight raid by the Federal Sensible Toys Bureau.

And so it was that I was given to attempt the occasional morning bath. Why did I not simply make this a routine slot in the schedule? Well, the morning bathing availability had competition with an event over which I had no control: the arrival of the Poop Fairies. I would never attempt to put a child in a tub if

I knew that it would coincide with a Regular Event, if you know what I mean. So, when a morning bath was desirable for other scheduling considerations, I would never lower her into the tub until the all clear sounded—or after I was relatively sure that the Poop Fairies had passed her over.

Now the bath I'm recalling must have been on one of those passover mornings. I know this for the same reason I can estimate how old my daughter was. It's because she was just verbal enough to say, "Uh-oh." The first thing I thought when she said it in the tub was how adorably cute her voice was. I was jolted from that reverie by the sudden realization of what that uh-oh meant.

I swooped her out of the tub and plopped her onto the toilet, where . . . nothing happened. False alarm. I waited for a minute or two for good measure, then restored her to the tub.

> **DADA DATA**
> **Amazing Dad Facts You Would Never Have Believed!**
>
> Hey, guys! Did you ever think it was possible to get tired of poop jokes?
>
> Guess what. It is!

My shoulder wasn't yet limber enough to pat myself on the back (see chapter 3 on hips), but I indulged in a self-congratulatory smirk before I noticed. You know danged well what I noticed, too. *Arrrgggh!*

I had no time to indulge my chagrin. I had to hoist her from the befouled bathwater, extract the offending matter, drain and disinfect the tub, then refill it, all the while trying to corral the wet and naked little perpetrator, lest she track God-knows-what germs around the house before she could be rebathed.

The only thing I was self-congratulatory about this time was the relative ease with which I scooped the poo from the water—not an easy task if you've ever tried it (and I know you have). You see, I got an A in Fluid Mechanics way back when I was studying for my aerospace degree.

And this is what I do with it. Fish turds out of the bathtub. Yeesh.

This is exactly why people get nostalgic about college. Back in those halcyon (the word means "ignorant;" go ahead and look it up) days, we didn't yet know the reality of what we would be doing with the theories we were learning. Perhaps it was the same with Byron, Blake, and Shelley. They failed to describe the realities of love because they had yet to live them to the fullest, not just because reality was unpoetic.

But my wife loves me with poetic passion for my ability and willingness to contend with these realities. And especially for not mentioning it too often.

CHAPTER 14

The B Word

No one wants to grow up. Except kids. But I'll leave that irony for some other time.

It's just that a lot of parent-age people can't seem to let go of being "cool." On one level I get it. I don't want to feel culturally irrelevant either. On another level I find it terribly, terribly sad.

Grown-ups who have actually grown up don't *need* cool. Cool is for kids. Cool is the tool young oppressors use to establish a social pecking order before any meaningful standards for a pecking order have had a chance to develop. It is a placeholder for actual accomplishment.

When you've done something with your life, you can laugh at cool. You can wear black socks with sandals and shorts. Not that I would recommend that.

One part of clinging to cool seems to be the B word.

You know the one: *buddy.* I never, ever use that word with my kids. I don't want to be their buddy, I want to be their dad.

It may be different with parents who aren't with their kids all day long. They don't have to be the round-the-clock disciplinarian-teacher-guide-guardian. Maybe being a buddy is a way to beef up the quality time when they're home from a hard day at work and need a respite from conflict. But as the quantity-time parent, I need to reserve my right to say, "Because I said so." A buddy can't

"Buddies don't give buddies time outs."

do that. Nor can a buddy be imposing enough to chase away the scary dreams. That takes a grown-up. A big, mean, scary, safe dad. The sort of a guy who would throttle any kid who tried to throw wood chips into his three-year-old's face at the playground and snarl, "That's *my* daughter," in his best Mean Dad voice and not give a crap about what anybody else thinks about it.

The downside to such stodgy authoritarianism is that my kids won't think I'm cool. Their friends won't think I'm cool. It reminds me of a car commercial I saw a few years ago. A mom was driving the babysitter home in the family van. The babysitter was prattling on about some teenage nonsense, who said what to whom or whut-ev-errr. Then she turned to the mom and said something like, "You're so lucky. You don't have to be cool anymore." Then came the shocker. Instead of whooping and hollering hallelujah, the mom's expression darkened with concern. "What?" her face seems to say. "I'm not cool? Nooooooo!" The announcer sidled in to offer the mom hope in the form of a cooler family vehicle.

Captain Dad Tot Tip:
Experts agree: When it comes to discipline, consistency is good.

Therefore, when you consistently urge your children to behave properly, that's good. Right? Right.

So it's not nagging, it's consistency!

Baffling. It's baffling that any sane adult wouldn't laugh this commercial off the air.

Look, I haven't cured cancer or even invented a better mousetrap. But I've held a job, bought a house, found a respectable wife, and raised kids. Any two of those provide me with enough sense of accomplishment that I don't need teenagers—let alone toddlers—to think I'm cool.

The way I look at it, I shouldn't be seeking their approval. They should be seeking mine.

It's not like I disagree with the cheerleaders of our child-centric culture. Children are indeed the future.

But!

We—their parents—are the *now.*

Their world should revolve around *us,* not the other way around. We're the ones with the car keys, not just because our legs are long enough to reach the pedals, but because we know our way around.

"Sometimes I wonder if it's worth all the pressure to have the whole world revolve around me."

When people tell kids that they are the Most Wonderful, Most Special, Most Important, Most Superlative children on the planet, I'm sure they are nothing but sincere. Heck, a reasonable amount of overblown praise is a good thing. My concern, however, is that amping up a kid's self-esteem too much, such as elevating him to buddy status, might fry his motherboard.

I don't mean to denigrate their little heads. I'm down with the gung-ho, goo-goo child advocates who croon, "Kids are *soooo* much smarter than you think!" The thing is, I think they're *soooo* smart that, even when they are acting like they don't need you and can do everything on their own, deep down they still know they're just kids.

Besides, however big their brains, they still have little shoulders. Too many superlatives are a lot of weight to lay on them.

Kids *are* special. So they deserve to be treated like . . . well, like children.

So, I call my girls things like *Sweetie, Cutie Cakes,* and *Baby Bones*. I'll even call them Princess. If only to remind them who I am—their king.

They'll have all the buddies they need in school. Buddies to play with, buddies to laugh with, buddies to try on "cool" with. But when times get tough, when they feel threatened by bullies or self-doubt—say, for not being cool enough—they'll know they can turn to Big Bad Dad to make them feel safe and tell them with absolute authority that they are loved and worthy of being loved.

And that's the best way I know to be their friend.

CHAPTER 15

Scientific Parenting

There was a playgroup at a local school that let pre-preschool kids come in one morning a week and share germs. As if that wasn't enough of an attraction, the moms and nannies got to sit around and . . . well, they got to sit around. That was the big draw. The room itself was not particularly large, but it was jam-packed with toys. An awesome playroom.

"Want to go to the park and work on your motor skills?"

But did they call it the Playroom? The Toy Room? The Crazy Little Squirrels Room? Nope. They called it—and I quote—The Motor Skills Room.

Welcome to the Age of Scientific Parenting.

Fun is no longer the purpose of toys, games, and entertainment. Everything has to promote cognitive development to make sure we have a world-class workforce for the jobs of the future. Programs may be "play-*based,*" but they can never be just play.

Even if it *is* just play, it can't be pitched that way. Going to a kiddie sing-along class? It has to advertise the benefits of music in support of math skills, coordination, and fine-motor control or no one will sign up.

Sleepology 101

Even putting the baby to bed comes swaddled in ideology. In fact it's no longer called "putting the baby to bed," it's called "sleep training." You are supposed to choose among Ferberizing (a.k.a. Sleep Nazism) and Cosleeping (a.k.a. *not* sleeping, because who can really sleep with a wriggly baby in the bed?), Cry-It-Out systems and No-Tears countersystems, and the Weissbluth Method and the Sleepeasy Solution—everything but the Hold-Them-Over-the-Gas-Jet-Why-Not-It-Worked-for-My-Father Method. Each, of course, comes with a book, a DVD, and worth-every-penny seminars you have to book months in advance. And the stakes are high. Choosing the wrong method can cost your child valuable IQ points. At least according to the brochures.

I'm working on a method myself. It's called the If-My-Parents-Weren't-So-Uptight-Maybe-I-Could-Get-to-Sleep Method. Only $1,740 for the two-day seminar (and a free DVD). Sign up today if you think you might get pregnant in the next thirty-six months.

The thing is, though, I don't blame parents for being a little uptight about their kids' sleep. A lot of sleep secrets can be very counterintuitive. Like, if you want your baby to sleep later in the morning so you don't have to crawl out of bed so dadgummed early, the logical thing to do would be to put your baby to bed later. Yes? *Ehhhhhhhtt.* Wrong answer. Put your baby to bed *earlier* to make her sleep later. Sounds crazy, but it works. As one seasoned mom explained it to me, sleep begets sleep.

Captain Dad Tot Tip:
You've heard how turning on a vacuum cleaner can help when a baby is crying uncontrollably. But did you know that the same trick works when the kids get older—and for the same reason? When they're whining and wailing about one thing or another, turn on the vacuum cleaner and it totally drowns out the noise!

Another counterintuitive freaky factoid is that when your kids get really tired, you can tell because they . . . (wait for it) have *more* energy. It's true. Extreme tiredness in kids triggers a release of adrenaline. So they get the crazies at the exact moment you want them to sleep. And if that keeps them from getting enough shut-eye tonight, you can count on the crazies having a sleepover so they can play at your house all day tomorrow.

According to the sleep charts, our younger daughter needs roughly a half hour more sleep than our older daughter. So we tried putting them to bed at the same time for a while, figuring the younger one would sleep a little longer in the morning. Then we couldn't figure out why she was melting down so often. Was it just a phase? If it was, it was an annoyingly long phase. Then we wondered, *Hmm, maybe she should go to bed . . . earlier? Ding ding ding!* Correct answer. The meltdowns cleared up literally overnight. And now we know that if she is cheated out of so much as a half hour's sleep at night, there will be hell to pay the next day.

Sleep charts. Live by them. It's science you can use.

Exactly *how* you get your kids to sleep, sorry, that's more of an art. Because science is something you can replicate. And what worked with the first child won't work with the second. For one thing, you didn't have another kid in the house when you had your first child. There was only one nap schedule to rule your day. There was only one bedtime ritual you had to observe. And chances are, by the time your second child showed up, the first one's bedtime ritual had evolved into something that would make a Greek Orthodox liturgist's head spin. But you can't do that anymore with both kids, not unless you start the ritual a few minutes after breakfast.

The second child, unfortunately, is typically sleep-disadvantaged. The younger sister can't have the same peaceful nap times, because her older sister is running around making too much noise. The younger sister wants to stay up later or get up

"He's really quite gifted, just not in any verifiable way."

earlier to see all the cool stuff the older one gets to do. Younger kids lose a lot of sleep. That's probably why studies show that second children usually have lower IQs than firstborns (and the third lower than that, and so on). And why the Chinese are so smart. It's not because of inherent math skills. It's because of their One Child Policy.

Study: Failure to Read This Book Could Lower Your Child's IQ by Ten Points

This all brings us to the great minefield of modern parenting: child cognitive development. There is a hungry market for programs

"Face it, lady. If he was an Einstein, you wouldn't be looking for a DVD."

and products that will transform your generally smart-enough kid into a supergenius. And we shell out the dough for it on the remote chance that it maybe, possibly might work just a teeny tiny bit. And if we don't buy it, everyone else who did will have an edge on us, which is unfair because our kids are the smartest, cutest, most superlative-in-every-way kids on the planet.

Besides, who knows? What if we really *can* boost our kid's IQs? We'd be fools not to try, right?

So we shell out the dough for things like Baby Einstein, which is among the most scientifish of them all. It was inspired by a study wherein students' spatial abilities seemed to improve while they listened to Mozart. Not Berlioz, not Beethoven, not Basie. Not even Meatloaf. Just Mozart. And it didn't help with math skills or vocabulary or logic puzzles. Just spatial reasoning. The media dubbed it the Mozart Effect.

Other scientists tried to replicate the study, with no success. The Mozart Effect, therefore, was an anomaly. That is, it didn't really exist.

But the name sure did, and that's all anyone saw in the papers. "The Mozart Effect!" One of those people extrapolated that classical music in general would therefore make babies smarter, contrary to the fine print in the Mozart Effect story. And contrary to the studies that debunked the Mozart Effect. But no one cared, and the Baby Einstein CDs—then books and DVDs—sold by the millions. Who wouldn't want their baby to be an Einstein?

We were given lots of these products as baby shower presents. The one book we still have teaches children that penguins live in the Arctic. Penguins, as you know, live in the Antarctic. Perhaps this sort of gaffe is why a later scientific study found that Baby Einstein DVDs actually stunted babies' language skills and mental development. The company was gracious enough to recall the videos, although if they were truly clever, they could have pointed out that Einstein himself didn't talk until he was three, so what did anyone expect?

Unfair Warnings

The overall effect on parents is sort of a post-traumatic stress disorder from all these attempts to cash in on our fears. First come the studies, then the subsequent studies that prove what chumps we were to fall for the original studies. If there needs to be one more study, let it be on the elevation of parental stress hormones due to all the other danged studies.

Seriously, Franklin Roosevelt said that all we had to fear was fear itself, and sure enough, there are now studies that prove the debilitating effects of fear. But Roosevelt was wrong about that being the *only* thing to fear. The list gets longer every day.

Crack open a newspaper or magazine, and some new fear leaps out and smacks you in the face (which is scary in itself). For instance, you grease up your child before letting her go outside because you already read about how photons from the sun should never come in contact with your child's skin (despite the resultant Vitamin D deficiency); but *now* you learn that the 100 percent organic, gluten-free, nut-free, dairy-free sunblock you've been putting on your baby might just as well be labeled

"I'm a Presbyterian whose mom ran out of sunscreen."

"Death Paste" from some heretofore unknown reaction between ingredients.

So you do the only sensible thing. You close your newspaper and turn on the radio. But out of it comes an ominous voice. "It rots wood, crumbles stone, reduces forged steel into dust . . ." Then you hear a whooshing sound; that's the blood draining from your head. ". . . and it's in the air your children breathe!" The room starts to spin, your heart hammers against your ribs, nearly drowning out the ghastly payoff. "It's *moisture*." (Piano chords of doom go here.)

You have been warned. Nothing is safe.

The constant pounding we get from the gloomsayers is enough to drive anyone crazy. Add to the mix that raising kids predisposes you to insanity in the first place, and you're guaranteed to get freaked out by the latest science report that something in sandwich bread will make your children's heads implode or cause their skin to fall off in sheets.

And you dare not let yourself get desensitized to these warnings, or you put yourself on the slippery slope to stuffing your kids with cigarettes and corn liquor.

On the whole, however, I suppose the legion modern childhood blights—from allergies and asthma to zits and zygomycosis—are probably preferable to the diphtheria and death that characterize what we call the Good Old Days. And "learning disguised as fun" is probably less soul sucking than slaving in a sweatshop at age four. But that doesn't mean these things aren't worth worrying about.

Of course, now that I've said that, just you watch. Tomorrow's paper will feature a study on how worrying leads to a slow, agonizing death.

Maybe it's the newspapers who should try to make learning fun.

CHAPTER 16

Ask Captain Dad!

Children are naturally curious. All the preschool handouts say so. And we are encouraged to encourage their curiosity. We want their curly little heads to be chock-full of questions.

Like, *Why do we say chock-full?*

Dads excel at answering such questions. As long as accuracy is not a factor. *Chock,* for example, sounds exactly like the way most kids pronounce the word *chalk.* Chalk, before it was used to deface sidewalks and help China reduce its glut of lead ore, was something teachers used to write with on large black slates called blackboards. Again, this was way before whiteboards and PowerPoint. If a day's lesson were going to be a big one, it would require lots of writing on the blackboard, hence a lot of chalk. Students knew that their heads were about to be crammed to the breaking point when they walked into class and saw the cup holding the chalk filled to overflowing. The cup was full. With chalk.

Their tiny kid brains, then, would likewise be *chalk-full* by the end of class. Or, in the more childlike pronunciation, *chock-full.* That's the way they learned the expression in their uneducated youth, and that's the way they passed it on to their even more ignorant juniors, and that's the way it survived once everyone had grown up. They simply forgot the saying's origins. Just as they forgot nearly everything else they learned in school. The fact that such a malapropism arose from the education process itself is indeed a sorry irony. But that's the way it is.

Ah, now I can practically hear some of you asking, "Wow, is that true?"

No! It's not! I made it up as fast as I could type it. Why? Because I'm a *guy.* Guys *do* that. If we don't know an answer, we BS our way through without missing a beat. Say anything with an air of authority, and people will believe you. Where do you think the entire profession of consulting came from? Men making stuff up! Women talk of the glass ceiling, but truth be told, it's a BS ceiling. Were women in better touch with their inner BS-er, then *they* would be running the big corporations. Into the ground. Just like their current male BS-er counterparts have done. But I digress. Which is yet *another* reason why dads excel in this area. Digression, like BS, is another great way to provide the illusion of substance without actual substance. Especially if it is a BS digression. But I digress on my digression.

Kids can't stop asking, *Why? Why? Why? Why?* It makes parents crazy, especially after they've answered the question ten times and done the same with each of the inevitable follow-up

questions until they're explaining the situation at the quantum level.

But!

A competent dad can BS his way through the dauntingest of Whys. Why? Because all we care about is having an answer that could pass as plausible to anyone less informed on the subject than we are. No matter how absurd it may be. In fact, we pride ourselves on the absurdity of our constructions. For instance, pick a for instance. Anything. Somebody, just shout it out.

Okay, I heard, *How come rain clouds are gray but other clouds are white?*

Electricity. The more electricity a cloud collects, the darker the cloud. That is why only the darkest clouds emit lightning and the fluffy white ones don't. How does it work? The same as liquid crystal display (LCD) flat-screen technology.

Remember your old pocket calculator? No? Okay, your first iPod? It had an LCD. Liquid crystals were laid out on a grid. When certain ones received an electrical charge, they turned black and spelled out numbers. Similar liquid crystals—we know them as snow, hail, sleet, and so on—make up clouds. (When the air below the clouds is warm, the crystals melt to rain.)

But the big question is, *Where does the electricity come from?* Us, mostly. We beam it into the air as radio and television signals, cell phone and satellite transmissions. (Cosmic radiation from alien sitcoms used to account for cloud darkening in prehistoric times.) Note how the increased use of these technologies coincides with global warming. Darkened clouds reflect less of the sun's heat. The more the talking heads on TV preach about global warming, the closer we are to a planet wiped out by scalding thunderstorms.

Now, after an explanation like that, the next time your curious wunderkind has a question, he or she might consider walking to the library and looking up the answer in a *book*.

And, for that, you can thank Captain Dad.

CHAPTER 17

The Other ADD

Orchids are rare and beautiful and delicate. People who raise them are passionate about them. Some people would compare them to children that way. I see you nodding along. Good. Now I can tell you my orchid story.

My wife, before she was my wife, never had much luck with orchids. She would dutifully mist them, water them, fertilize them, sing to them. But the orchids failed to flourish. When she met me, I had a dozen or so orchids (thanks to a buddy in the greenhouse business who kept unloading them on me). She marveled at my ability to make them thrive and rebloom. Finally she asked me how I did it. Here's my secret, exactly as I told it to her: I put them in a corner of the house that gets the right light, and I water them in the sink for one minute once a week.

That's it.

Some things, you see, flourish with just the right amount of neglect. Kids, for instance.

Hey, don't look at me like that. *You* agreed they were like orchids! And it's true. Kids need neglect. In the right measure, that is. Think of it as something you can excel at. A confidence builder.

But it takes surprising effort. Because the natural tendency is to want to protect your precious little flower every second of

"You just come home and neglect her at night. I'm the one who has to neglect her all day."

the day, even though you know that if you do, then he'll never develop the strength to blossom on his own. Or to resolve conflicts with his sister.

I wish I had learned sooner that if I left my girls alone in the playroom together—with me out of sight—they got along better. There was no one's attention to compete for. But the moment I'd poke my head around the corner, "Daddy! She's being mean to me!" "I am not! You stole my . . ." You know the routine, probably better than you know "Who's on First."

Other benefits I have found are, if I studiously ignore them long enough, say, to clear the dishes out of the sink, I might find them reading a book on their own. Or I'll walk into the playroom later only to be yelled at, "Aaahhh! You're walking in the water! Quick, get on the boat!"

Unfortunately you can only get away with so much detachment parenting before your child's ADD reasserts itself. No, I'm not talking about that other attention deficit disorder. I'm talking about the one that demands *your* attention. Tons of it. All of it. More than you may have to give.

Like the TV at my neighbor's house, you're always on.

Even when the kids seem like they are off doing their own thing, you know the line: "Dad, look at *me!*" "Mom, watch *this!*"

Haven't you ever wanted to have a form letter in your pocket for these occasions?

Dear [son or daughter's name goes here],

Yes, I saw you [do that thing that you did]. It was great. A world record! I never imagined anyone could [do that thing] so amazingly. And to think, it was your first time ever!

I notice all the amazing things you do. And there are so many that it's hard to keep them all straight. Which is why I may have to stop and think really hard when you ask me questions like, "Remember that time I was on my tricycle and we came to that huge bump?" Sure, I remember, but it takes a few seconds to find that particular memory among the gazillion others. Which would explain the blank look you see on my face.

So don't you worry. I'm always looking, always paying attention. I could have no other thoughts than of you. Even if I tried.

Attentively yours,
[Mom/Dad]

I like to imagine the two-minute mental vacation I'd enjoy while my daughter read that letter (at least the reading-aged one). Except I know I'm just imagining. In the real world it would be, "Read it to me! . . . Again! . . . Again!"

"I had a scary dream that I wasn't getting any attention."

As a parent it is all too easy to succumb to attention fatigue. But I own a graying chocolate bunny as a cautionary reminder of what can happen during a momentary lapse.

It was around the time Lucy outed Grammy for feeding her chocolate. Lucy was on either side of her second birthday. We were in Target. Some weary, attention-depleted parent must have had her back turned for a moment in the candy section. Some time later she evidently apprehended her child with a contraband Easter bunny, whereupon she wrested it from his hands and plunked it back on a shelf.

Not the candy shelf, of course. A faraway shelf. *Any* shelf.

I envision the tap dance she had to perform to prevent the publicly humiliating meltdown. "Oh, but Sweetie, Mr. Bunny and all the Mr. Piggies are friends. Thank you for bringing Mr. Bunny to visit them. No, Sweetie, he wants to be among all the nice piggy banks. So that's where we'll leave Mr. Bunny. Oh, look! SpongeBob sweatpants—way over there!"

Overheard on the Playground:

"His last nanny was Romanian, so all he says is 'da.'"

Then, with that not-so-subtle misdirection, she zoomed the cart away, leaving the bunny behind on some random shelf, among the brightly colored piggy banks, miles from the special Easter candy section, where no one would ever expect to find a chocolate bunny.

Or, more precisely, where no one would ever expect their two-year-old daughter to find a chocolate bunny. In fact some

"My wife and I used to joke about our older daughter's seeming inability to hear us. But when her doctor asked about her hearing, she cheerily volunteered, 'I have a listening problem.'"

poor sap might even presume that the shelf full of colorful plastic piggy banks was an ideal misdirection, something harmless that could hold his little girl's attention for twenty seconds while he attempted to find a particular strain of light bulb among today's myriad bewildering options.

That sap was me.

Twenty seconds later, with bulb in hand, the metaphoric bulb inside my head seemed to need replacing, since for the life of me I could not figure out what that brown stuff smeared all over my little girl's face was.

Not only had she found a strange object and determined it to hold chocolate inside—despite it being completely sealed in gold foil—but she had gnawed her way through the foil wrapper and devoured half the ears. In twenty seconds.

Now I had to pay for the danged thing. I flashed a cheesy grin to deflect the checkout clerk's judgmental eyes as she swiped the slobbery remains ever so delicately across the scanner. I thought to offer her a wet wipe, but I had spent my entire supply mopping the evidence off of my daughter's face.

My next problem was that I didn't want my would-be shoplifter to think that all she had to do was bite the head off of something and Daddy would automatically buy it for her. I had to explain to her how wrong she was to do that, but not so forcefully that she wouldn't forget about the bunny on the way home. It was critical that she forget about the bunny. I couldn't reward her misdeed by letting her eat the rest of it, but I didn't want to have to listen to her screaming for twenty minutes to test my resolve. So now *I* was the parent who had to hide it and move on. I had to wait for a lapse in her attention. Which, as you know, isn't easy.

So I said to her, "Why don't you clean up this playroom a little. And could you put these books away? Then, when you're done with that . . . Lucy? . . . Lucy?"

Sigh.

What else could I do? That's the only way to make sure kids won't pay attention to you.

Would It Be So Wrong...?

Would it be so wrong if one were to invent any of these parenting conveniences?

- **The Night Muzzle**: For the kid who has trouble closing both his eyes *and* his mouth.
- **Velcro Pajamas with Matching Sheets**: Just don't throw away all those nighttime pull-ups quite yet.
- **Lead Soled Shoes**: "They're jumpless!"
- **GPS Tracker Implant**: Because kids wander off, and an invisible fence with shock collar *would* be wrong. Ditto the plutonium tag with the Geiger counter tracker.
- **Shampoo Helmet**: It covers their hair and seals out everything else. Then you add water and shampoo, and you can wash their hair without them screaming about getting water in their eyes.

- **MagnaCuffs**: A magnetic tether that invisibly binds them to you in public places. Avoids all the judgmental looks associated with the kiddie leash.

- **Soundproof Privacy Window for the Family Car**: Kind of like the ones they have in taxis and limos. Ah, sweet silence.

- **Sleepie Lite**: You know those nightlights that emit air freshener? Well, this is one of those, except it fills their bedroom with a gentle mist of ether.

CHAPTER 18

Captain Chopped Liver

I sympathize with those supposedly vapid housewives circa 1957. It's not that they were vapid, they just sounded that way. I know because I'm becoming one of them, except with chest hair.

My wife comes home at night with talk of her day, meeting Very Important People and talking about Very Important Things. Even the things she does *without* capital letters seem fast paced and exotic.

And what do I say about *my* day? "Lucy used the word *humongous* today." I remember that, when Lucy had just turned three. I thought it might sound fairly impressive. "Ooh, that's great, Lucy," my wife chirped supportively, "I'm so proud of you!" Back to me. "What was it about?" I could have offered to show her; it was still in the diaper bin. Or not. I decided instead to make something up. I tried to say . . .

Uh, I don't know. I went blank. Even now I can't think of anything clever. Talking to toddlers all day, about humongous poops and which one of us is Ariel this time and can ants really talk, does not do scintillating things for the old brain box. So I shrugged and said, "Oh, I can't remember." Which was painfully plausible.

Then I let my wife go on about her day of Saving the World from the Forces of Evil and Other Capitalized Stuff. It's not that

I'm jealous. I have my own capital-lettered job too, after all. Staying home with the kids, as the saying goes, is The Most Important Job in the World, isn't it? But—let's be honest—as another saying goes, *It doesn't take a rocket scientist.*

Take it from me. As you may recall, I used to be one. And the closest I ever came to using those skills was in that episode of figuring the most efficient way to fish a wayward turd out of the bathtub.

But even my vapid little mind can surmise that this particular discourse on fluid mechanics would fail to impress at the dinner table. So what do I do to assert my Importance? What do I say to sound Interesting? "I weighed the crumbs I swept from under the table today. Four and a half ounces!" Or, "I meant to get more bananas today, but on our way home from school we saw a kitty cat! And everyone got to pet it!" Or, "I managed to fit that last coffee mug into the dishwasher when it looked like you couldn't cram in so much as another kiddie spoon." Okay, there's another way I've used my engineering degree. Whoop-ti-do.

I just want to have something to contribute. Those 1950s housewives could at least bouf up their hair and put on high heels and an *au courant* frock. They could simply look good. Husbands fall for that sort of thing. But I have a *wife.* She's going to know I've totally lost it if I put my hair up in a beehive. Not that I have the hair left to do it anyway.

So all I can do is just sit there. Maybe nod sympathetically here and there. Murmur, "Mm-hmm," or, "Uh-huh." But I can't really *say* anything. I can only listen.

Hold on.

Give me a moment here. I think I'm about to have an epiphany. It's coming . . . it's coming . . .

(*Ding!*) It's here!

I can . . . listen. Yes! I remember hearing somewhere that women actually *like* it when men listen. Just *listen.* They hate when men are always trying to cut in with something More Important to say. At least I think so. I'm not 100 percent sure. I heard it way back when I had things to say myself, so I wasn't really listening.

But that's it. I can become interest*ing* by being interest*ed.* Then—I know this much—my wife will talk about it to the other wives she works with. And oh, brother, will they listen! Next thing you know they will mention it to *their* husbands and ask why they can't be more like *my wife's* husband. And then all those high-powered important dudes will actually feel *threatened* by me.

Which is all I really want. To feel like I still matter.

Except . . .

I know that I matter only so much. There's a limit. One minute I can feel like I really am Captain Dad. The next, it's Captain Chopped Liver.

Sure, I'm the go-to guy with the kids. I'm there for them around the dial, every day. Every messy meal, every dirty diaper. I sit through endless tea parties. I gamely play hide-and-seek in rooms that have no legitimate hiding places, but still I pretend

"Your father's the one to talk to about crippling disappointment."

that I can't see the giggling lump under the sofa cushions. I kiss every boo boo when they cry, "I hurt my finger! Kiss my finger!" Even that time one of my daughters fell on her backside and squealed, "I hurt my butt! Kiss my butt!" and I dutifully kissed it, holding back my own laughter because of her tears, knowing she wouldn't get the joke and would only be more hurt. I've picked up after them endlessly and yelled at them to pick up after themselves nearly as much. I've hugged them after time-outs and have run to their room at night when they were scared and so Mommy wouldn't be a wreck at work the next day by having to haul herself out of bed at three in the morning. And again at four-thirty.

And when they were feeling sick and miserable, I wiped the boogers, squeezed droppers of Purple Juice into them, listened patiently to their litany of symptoms, and soothed and sympathized as they called out over and over . . .

"I want my mommy!"

Or as my younger daughter used to say when she was still itty-bitty, "Be mommy! Be mommy!"

That's right, my brothers, you may think that that stream of projectile vomit was meant for you. And it may sting at first to learn it wasn't. But if you're man enough to be a Captain

Dad, you're man enough to get that it isn't personal. It's something primal. It's in our genes.

No, I don't mean that women are inherently better at holding the barf bowl or that men feel their children's pain any less. It's just that it doesn't matter how old you are, when you're down, and I mean way down—picture Daffy Duck with his bill and feathers blown off—only a mommy can comfort you.

Stay-at-home dads may change plenty about gender roles in our society, but we'll never change that. And I pray we'll never have the hubris to want to.

And I pray that the moms who for one reason or another can't be with their little ones 25/8 (at least, it *feels* more than 24/7) won't ever doubt how much they matter to their children. Moms are the bedrock of their existence, their tether to this earth.

What can I say? It's a mom's world. I would never take that away from my wife. I'll just swallow my pride and accept it. And I'm okay with that. Because it is Something Important that I can actually do.

Sacrifice

We all like to believe that we are willing to make sacrifices for our children. But we often doubt we will be able to when the time comes.

Don't worry. You *will* be able to do it. Just you wait.

There will come a time when you see your eighteen-month-old tearing the pages out of that *New Yorker* article you actually intended to read for six weeks but have yet to find the time. When she starts shredding the pages into identity-theft-prevention–size bits, will you shriek at her to stop? Or will you make that sacrifice for ten minutes of relative calm?

Sacrifice.

Or you may see your just-turned-toddler crawl into the shower. You will instantly envision the eighteen different ways she could slip and scramble her brains all over the tub, and you will want to rush to save her. Yet you will make that sacrifice—for five minutes of knowing that she is in a confined space and you do not have to chase her all over the house.

Sacrifice. Sacrifice.

Or when you're trying to load the kids in the car and they are crying out for brownies. You will want to tell them, "No. You're on your way to Grammy's house. There are always treats at Grammy's house." And you know it wouldn't be fair to deliver the kids all amped up on sugar, but it's a long drive to Grammy's house and they are still crying for those blasted brownies. So what will you do?

Sacrifice. It's what makes a good parent great.

CHAPTER 19

The Science and Stress of Being a Stay-at-Home Dad

There was a day some months back when everybody I encountered would ask me, "How are you feeling? You feeling alright?" I'd say I'm fine, and they'd breathe a sigh of relief, and we'd act like nothing happened. But I could still see the concern in their eyes. I didn't know what was going on until, on a hunch, I started searching the Internet for "stay-at-home dad," since that was about all these people knew about me.

On the very first page of my search was an article about some recent scientific study about the stress of being a stay-at-home dad. A team of scientists tracked the health of thirty-six hundred people in Massachusetts for ten years. The relevant nugget from their research was

that stay-at-home dads had a much higher death rate—mostly from heart disease—than working dads. How much is much? 82 percent. That's a lot of much. It meant I could be working a high-pressure job on Wall Street, trying to pillage the world economy—*again*—while shielding myself from the siege of conscience . . . and it would be like an all-expenses-paid vacation in Tahiti compared to changing diapers and sweeping up crumbs all day.

A number of scientists chimed in with theories as to why this was. This is what scientific circles call "peer review." The operative word is *peer*. In other words, these are all people who work in lab coats for a living. Lab coats curiously unmarred by yogurt stains and sticky little handprints, such as scientists who stayed home with kids and actually knew something about the subject matter might wear.

Peer review, however, is not the same as Captain Dad review. I, after all, have some genuine perspective from the trenches of stay-at-home dadhood. So let's consider these theories:

Theory Number One: Parents Eat What Their Kids Eat

Even a healthy kids' diet is packed with high-sodium, high-fat foods like mac and cheese and hot dogs. There is only so much a kid's palate will tolerate, try as you may to make asparagus look tantalizing. Meanwhile, it can be hard for parents to find time to prepare two separate meals, one for the kids and one for themselves. So they end up eating a lot of artery-clogging goo they'd never touch if they had older dining companions. And they frequently eat even more of it than they intended to, by salvaging the uneaten bits instead of letting so much go to waste—a problem that has been plaguing moms' waistlines since the invention of processed food.

"Hmm," I hear you say. "That sounds reasonable. What could possibly be wrong with such an obvious theory?" Well . . . nothing. Except for the fact that this is a theory that the scientists did *not* think of—no matter how obvious it is to anyone who has ever spent more than a day around kids. I mention it to underscore my point about the scientists perhaps being out of touch.

Now, to really drive that point home, let's look at what they *did* come up with. No more fake-outs, I promise.

Theory Number Two: Men Underestimate How Difficult the Job of Staying Home with the Kids Is

Okeydoke. Some scientist actually thought that this theory was clever. And his or her "peers" thought it worthy of serious consideration. So, hmm, let's consider it, too.

Yes, okay, I can see a man underestimating the job. On Day One. But this was a *ten-year* study! Unless all of these 82 percent more croakers were keeling over on the first day, I think they'd catch on to the fact that they had better recalculate their expectations—and do it well before nap time.

But, to be scientific about it, let's conduct what's called a "mind experiment" (what scientists use when they have limited funding). Imagine, for the sake of science, deliberately pouring boiling water into your lap because you "underestimate" how hot

"Duh!"

it will be. Now put the kettle back on the stove to get it back to full steam. And do it again. Gosh, did you think it could really be that hot . . . a *second* time? Nope? Still not convinced? Okay, try it again. And again. And again. How many times do you imagine it will take before you formulate the theory that the steaming, roiling, blistering water will be uncomfortable if poured into your crotch?

From our mind experiment I think we can infer that whatever preconceptions you *began* stay-at-home dadding with will be beaten out of you mighty quick. Even if you're as thick as flies on a fertilizer farm—or a scientist's peer—you're likely to catch on.

This theory, then, is more likely a case of the *scientists* underestimating how *obviously* difficult the job is.

Look, I'm sure it's stressful being a scientist, writing grants, pleasing your peers, and managing a cadre of eager young grad students to do all of your grunt work. But to understand what stress can really be like, let's look at a common experience that a scientist might not view as stressful, but a stay-at-home dad might, because of the abjectly different ways we experience them. How about a phone call to the bank. These calls invariably come at an awkward time for everybody. But the scientist breezily brushes it off.

"Pardon the noise. My lab assistants are conducting some experiments with a rare viral strain endemic to macaque monkeys. I'll ask them to keep it down. Yes, the monkeys, too. Ha, ha." Ooh, imagine how embarrassing that must be for the scientist to have to admit this circumstance to the banker.

Hmm, come to think of it, maybe I should try that line myself. Mental note: "Macaque monkeys." I only hope the banker isn't savvy enough to distinguish the sound of little kids merely *screaming* like monkeys from the sound of actual monkeys.

Not that my kids are always screaming. They actually play delightfully together most of the time. Until the phone starts ringing. That's like a cosmic trigger for one kid to whack the other with a magic fairy wand, or to pick up a toy that neither has played with for weeks but now *at this very instant* neither can resist. That's when the wailing begins.

Which means my cover is blown. The banker on the other end of the phone now knows that I am not in my grown-up professional laboratory but at home with the kids. So he speaks more slowly. He makes little attempt to hide the strained sympathy in his voice. He may even go so far as to say, "Oh, yeah. I remember those days." Except what he probably really remembers is the brief parts of the day when he was home from work and the kids were getting ready for bed. Or the weekends when he couldn't escape to the golf course. And he had to pick them up at the regular time from day care. Because I swear to you that I have talked with a banker who kept her kids in day care on her days off so she could actually enjoy her days off. So forgive me if "Oh, yeah, I remember" doesn't exactly strike a chord of solidarity with me. To me it sounds more like, "Oh, you poor schmuck."

It's not that I'm insecure in my masculinity or self-worth. Much. But little things like this can grind on anyone. Especially when it doesn't stop with the phone calls. It's with other things, too. Anything. Everything.

Even the simplest things. The naturalest things. Things you would ordinarily associate with relief—not stress. Things that normal adults in the workplace get to do with no more hassle than simply barking, "Hold my calls for five minutes."

Me, I can't count on anyone to hold anything for five minutes. Case in point: My daughter had a playdate. The kids were happily romping in the yard when I thought it would be safe to enjoy a moment's relief.

Suddenly I heard the patio door fling open. The playdate companion came running in—in need of the bathroom! From the urgency of the door flinging, I could instantly assess the situation. There was a clatter of feet across the floor and a rattling of the door handle. All I needed was two more seconds to pull up my pants. Two seconds! Okay, five, tops.

They make energy drinks. But what I need is a patience drink.

No good. Too late. I opened the door and saw that I had to get out the mop. And not simply for the tears gushing from this humiliated four-year-old. Her mother, of course, was equally mortified when I handed over her daughter with the plastic bag of soaked garments.

She mustered her dignity and promised to return the loaner duds we let her daughter change into. "Keep them," I said. No one needed the reminder.

Situations like that are stressful enough to induce heart disease, but you know what's even more stressful? The constant interference with a person's intestinal regularity. Or the constant fear of interference. How come the scientists don't run a study on *that?*

Theory Number Three: Stay-at-Home Dads Have Less of a Support System Than Moms Do

Ding-ding-ding! Score one for the scientists.

Absolutely. Lack of a support group is a tremendous stress.

We Captain Dads are far fewer in number than female caregivers (moms, grandmas, aunts, and nannies). Most of the women we encounter are cordial to us, but we simply aren't "one of the girls." So we tend to be outside the automatic playdate circle. In other words, we are left on the fringe of the herd, to be picked off by those predators, Stress and Heart Disease.

But thanks to a couple of factors, that is changing, however slowly. First of all, the decimation of the global economy has been a boon to us. Lots more of us dads are now out there on the playground during business hours. You can thank Goldman-Sachs for that bit of social progress. Tack another zero onto those bonuses.

Also, the Internet has been a great, male-friendly tool to connect guys stressed out by their solitude and financial concerns with other guys who might also be looking for a way to decompress during nap times. All you have to do is type "stay-at-home dads" into a search engine, and in nano-seconds you are presented with . . .

. . . articles telling you that being a stay-at-home dad *will kill you.*

As if we needed anything else to give us heart failure!

CHAPTER 20

The Hunter, the Lamb, and the Walrus

Men were born to hunt. You just have to watch us shopping to know.

At the grocery store we have a list. If it's not on the list, it ain't coming home. (We also have a mental list for things like beer, chips, salsa, and cereal. So don't go crying gotcha if you spot a guy snagging one of these items not on the written list.) But our hunting grounds extend far beyond the grocery store. There is also the hardware store, where the prey can be more elusive. Like . . . well, it's a kind of a bolt—I don't know what you call it—but it has a roundish head and seems to be not quite thirty-two threads per inch so I don't know, maybe it's metric?

Some men even hunt for venison, but face it, that's just an outdoorsy version of grocery shopping.

However, if a man wants a *real* hunt; a good, old-fashioned hunt; a savage, spoors-in-the-woods, pulse-pounding-with-primal-terror *animal* hunt, then he should test his mettle on the Captain Dad Bedtime Safari.

It is a hunt where failure is worse than death. And success gives you no trophy to stuff and hang over your mantel. Because the beasts you seek are already stuffed.

In our house, there are two such beasts.

The very words, "Where's Lamby?" or "Where's Walrus?" are enough to sump the blood out of my head. I'd sooner stalk a wounded rhino, armed with no more than a day-old corn muffin and a ballpoint pen.

Stuffed animals are wily. They blend into the herds of other toys. They have an instinct for the unlikeliest places to be found. Unexpected rooms, improbably high shelves, the inside of bags or boxes or backpacks you didn't think anyone ever played with.

But their most harrowing habit is the hour at which they always choose to go afield. Bedtime. The hour when everyone is weary. Bedtime. When a meltdown can be triggered by the

subtlest tic at the quantum level. Bedtime. When everyone's attention should be directed toward . . . hmm, I don't know—how about *going to bed?*

And when I say at bedtime, I mean *at* bedtime. Not twenty minutes *before* bedtime, when you're not yet stressed to the bejeezus at the prospect of another bloody delay. If you're any kind of parent, you *know* to budget an extra twenty minutes for the stalling while undressing or playing with the water while brushing teeth until you have to count to five in that threatening tone. An extra twenty minutes for another glass of water, another song, another book, another kiss that you couldn't give away with the bribe of candy any other time of day. Twenty for the uncontrollable need to change jammies twice (not counting the soaked-jammies change necessary after the teeth-brushing water play), for the imperative to tell a secret (coded in gibberish), and for all the other predictable filibusters against bedtime. You budget for that. And there are nights when you reasonably think that you have everything under control, that tonight—tonight!—is the night when bedtime will actually be *at* bedtime!

Until . . . "Lamby!" "Walrus!"

I remember one time when Lamby went missing. Not just missing, but milk-carton missing. We had always feared such a tragedy, but we thought we were prepared for it. Once there was a clear choice of who the Superfriend would be of all our daughter's stuffies, we had the foresight to buy a duplicate stuffed lamb. But a carbon copy was no match for the discerning eyes of a not-yet-two-year-old. She wailed and rejected the unsoiled impostor. So we redoubled our efforts to pry up the floorboards if necessary and find the Real Thing.

Another time, we left for a three-day trip without Walrus. I realized this on the way to the train station. There was no time to drive back to get him. I pulled out my phone. Luckily Grammy was not far from our house and had a key. I made the outrageous request that she overnight Walrus to our motel. But that's not Grammy's way. She adores her granddaughter. She sent it same-day express. It arrived at our motel before bedtime. (Go, Grammy.)

The stakes are that high. Every night. Even when my patience was shot to pieces hours ago, my last nerve flapping above my skin like the tattered banner in some Revolutionary War propaganda sketch. Too bad. Stuffed animals have no mercy. Mercy lies in my hands alone.

Before me lies only the hunt, or there will be no rest in this house. Ever.

So back I go, down, down, down. Down to the heart of darkness. To hunt for Lamby or Walrus. Wishing it were a wooly mammoth. Or a saber-toothed tiger. Or that wounded rhinoceros—a *real* one. Any large, ferocious, living beast would be soooo much easier to find in the wilds of our family room.

The Nuclear Option

What if you threw a nuclear bomb and nobody blew up?

I ask because one night my wife and I had had enough. The playroom was a mess. No amount of gentle coaxing, positive reinforcement, nagging, hectoring, badgering, threatening, or yelling could get the kids to pick up after themselves and leave the room suitable for human habitation for five minutes afterward. We seriously contemplated calling FEMA. But then we remembered Hurricane Katrina and figured we'd better tend to this ourselves.

Our only choice left was the nuclear option. As soon as the girls went to bed, we pulled out a shopping bag and started filling it. Anything on the floor went into the bag. It didn't matter how new or precious the toy was. If it was on the floor, it was in the bag. Very soon we had to face a major flaw in our plan: We needed more bags.

Princess gloves, cards, plastic dolls, paper dolls, game pieces, puzzle pieces, stickers and crayons and papers and pens, toy food, real food, stuffed animals (mercifully no real animals), boxes and bags and purses, and so many things I don't even known the names of. All of it. Gone. We hauled it away to the dreaded Monday Box.

The Monday Box is where we used to take things that were left on the floor where they shouldn't be. Really we just hid them in the storage room (where we hide our own junk). The idea was that they wouldn't get the stuff back until the following Monday, and then maybe they'd learn. Oh, yes, we said to ourselves, they'd learn.

Except they didn't, of course. So we dropped the Monday Box for a while. Until that fated night, when it came back with a vengeance. And the floor of that playroom went from chaotic to desolate, like the wake of a neutron bomb.

We steeled ourselves for the morning's air-raid siren wails of outrage. They'd cry, not unfairly, that we were being inconsistent, though they wouldn't use those exact words. They'd throw fits about the princess gloves that were a gift from their Grammy only a week ago and how very cherished and beloved they were and how it was the only way they could feel close to Grammy while she is on vacation for a couple of weeks. They'd make up reasons far beyond my own creativity. My wife and I would expect the police to show up at our door because of all the uproar.

Night passed.

Morning came. My older daughter had gotten up first and I found her sitting on the stairs reading. She walked downstairs

with me, and I fed her some breakfast. A little later her sister woke up and came down. The two of them scampered off to the playroom. Then . . . ?

The sound was deafening. At least, that's how I interpreted it. Because I literally did not hear a thing.

Not a squeak, not a yelp, not the slightest acknowledgement that anything was different at all! They simply didn't notice.

So here's an idea. Maybe we should skip the threats. Just steal away the toys, one by one, until there are so few that they *can't* mess up the room. Will they *ever* notice?

Yes. They probably will. They will notice that a particular pack of stickers is missing. Or one scrap of paper they were using as a treasure map. In other words, the stuff that looked so insignificant that we didn't even bother with the Monday Box but threw it directly into the garbage.

Then they'll go nuclear.

CHAPTER 21

Wagon, Ho!

I'm dating myself here, but when I was a kid, parents said crazy things like, "Go outside and play." And we were crazy enough to do it. We'd run next door to see if the kids there were out. If they weren't, we'd stand at the back door and yell, "Ma-A-A-arrrk!" Unless the kid who lived there had a different name, of course. Then he'd come running out, and we'd hop on our bikes and go do something unspeakably dangerous, this being ten years before the invention of the bicycle helmet.

Today kids pester their parents to set up a playdate for them and then drive them there. Or take an extra kid or two home with them after school. And this is where the problem arises.

We have two kids, which means we have two booster seats in the back of our car. But it's a midsize sedan, which means that we're maxed out for legal child transport. I've been known to smuggle a child in the space between the boosters, but felt more like a human trafficker than a carpooler and slunk through back alleys for fear of being busted.

So we need a new car. Our children's social life depends on it. We want something that can carry our two kids plus one friend each. It may not look like a big problem on the face of it, but surprisingly it is.

Sedans max out at three backseat passengers, and precious few truly hold three booster seats. So what about an SUV? Oddly enough most SUVs *also* max out at three, which makes you wonder why the heck you'd want to deplete the education fund for the extra gas. Our family is not long in the inseam either, so climbing in and out of an SUV is pretty much a deal breaker. Nor can we avoid the inseam problem by wearing a skirt. My wife has ripped too many skirts trying to high step into other people's SUVs; and I look like hell in a kilt. Meanwhile, we still wouldn't be able to pack four kids into it. Unless we got the humungo-size land-crushing Planet Killer variety. And built a Jetway onto our house so we could get into the danged thing.

Which leaves us with the minivan. Clearly I am out of the closet as a domestic dad, so the concept shouldn't, and doesn't, bother me. Fuddy-duddy, thy name is Captain Dad. But someone at the car companies is *not* so sanguine with his Dockers dowdiness and has tried to make the contemporary minivan a skosh more macho (*skosh* being one of those words wannabe macho guys use). Consequently minivans now have the same entry-height issue. Arguably this is not an insurmountable

problem, but it does not appreciably improve one's quality of life to curse the stupidity of one's culture each time one stumbles in and out of one's vehicle.

So what do we do to get that one extra kid in the car and preserve our sangfroid? "Aha!" you say. "A station wagon!"

Of course. A station wagon. Why didn't we think of that? Station wagons were *invented* to carry buckets of kids.

Why, when I was a kid, you'd run out of kids before you'd run out of room in a station wagon. The whole baseball team and a relief pitcher could fit in there. I'm not kidding. Four kids in the backseat, two in the front, and four more in the rear. If you folded down the seats in the way back, you could stack kids like cord wood and take the opposing team out for ice cream as well.

So we went shopping for a station wagon. We asked how many people it would carry. The answer was five. Five people. Station wagons *these days* carry *five people.*

Five? No, no, no. There had to be some mistake. "What if we fold down the rear seats?" we asked. Ah, that was the secret question we had neglected to ask. If we fold down the rear seats, that would make a difference of three passengers. "Okay," we said, rubbing our hands together. "Now we're getting somewhere. So it's eight passengers, is it?"

No. The difference swings the other way. With the seats down, it's only two.

"Station wagon" is apparently the new term for "boxy hatchback." Which itself is a mere euphemism for "sedan with a window in the trunk so people can peek to see if there's anything good to break in and steal."

But wait, there's more. Rather, less. Most of those modern station wagons only hold five when the backseat is not cannibalized by booster seats. With booster seats, the passenger count drops to four.

"Oh, come on," I can hear you say. "Surely there is a station wagon that fits more than four. Or even five."

Fine. You got me. There *is* a station wagon like that. *A* station wagon. One—count 'em—one wagon on the market today has what they call "third-row seating." So it holds a whopping six passengers. Two adults and four kids. And if you can live without any options, it sells for only around $58,000.

I could build a time machine for less than that. And I'd have four thousand dollars left over to buy a brand-spanking-new

"How much is that in years of tuition?"

1967 Ford LTD station wagon, complete with spiffy imitation wood paneling, to bring back with me.

And we call this progress? Are the car companies simply trying to sell more cars? If you go beyond your allotted 2.3 children, you have to buy another car? And what do modern station wagons offer us in return for the inability to legitimately carry largish families in them, other than an iPod dock and cup holders?

So I'm building my time machine. I'm going back for my woody wagon. Screw the cup holders. I'll suffer through my kids and their many friends singing "B-I-N-G-O" as they spill their drinks all over the seats. Who cares? The seats are vinyl. They'll clean right up.

CHAPTER 22

Everything You Need to Know About Kids: They're Crazy

Erma Bombeck was right. Einstein was . . . well, not exactly wrong, per se; but he was no Erma Bombeck, that's for sure.

You all know the old Albert Einstein definition of insanity, to wit, "Doing the same over and over again and expecting different results."

But how does that apply to a world where doing the same thing over and over again *does* produce different results?

Because it does happen. For instance, I have a child who didn't like corn. Corn! What person on the planet could possibly not like corn, especially one from a corn-growing state? It's sweet, it's delicious, it comes on a cob. This kid would *ask* for broccoli. How could she not like corn? Talk about crazy!

What could we do but surrender to insanity? Which means we kept putting corn in front of her, expecting a different result. Until—finally!—we got one. Today, she eats corn. Loves it. Asks for it by name. *Now* who's crazy? Huh, Mr. Smarty-Pants?

Einstein would have had us abandon our insanity. It took a greater genius to embrace it within a more empirical worldview. Erma Bombeck.

It was she who famously posited, "Insanity is hereditary. You can catch it from your kids." Why she did not receive a Nobel

"You've all got your jackets on?
Great. Let's go."

Prize for that single observation is a mystery for future geniuses to ponder.

The point is Einstein, lost in his theoretical world, missed this little tidbit of reality. Kids are . . .

Look, I'm sorry. I know the ramifications of what I am about to say. I know you love your kids and you would never say anything bad about them or allow anyone else to say anything bad about them, but . . .

They're crazy. You know that, right?

How else do you explain them fighting over the heel of a loaf of bread but crying bloody murder if you fail to trim the crust from their sandwich?

Crazy. So you dutifully cut the crust off the next sandwich you make.

And they cry that they wanted it *on* this time.

Or when they want *you* to flush the toilet because the noise is scary—until you walk by a bathroom with an unflushed toilet and you do the only sensible (and sanitary) thing, only to have your toddler scamper in from two rooms away shrieking that *she* wanted to flush it this time.

Or you go to the park with the dozen or so exciting water features for kids (code name: the Crazy Water Park), and what does your toddler fall under the thrall of but the drinking fountain! The other, meanwhile, sits giggling as a four-inch pipe drains endlessly onto her head. Yes, the very same child who screams bloody murder about getting her hair wet to get it washed.

No rhyme. No reason. The only predictable result is that you will lose if you try to guess what they'll want or what's going to set them off. It's a nonstop ride on the crazy-go-round. What kept the peace last time won't work this time. What they devoured last week for lunch they won't touch today.

Doing the same thing over again *always* produces a different result. At least in Parent World.

So why *wouldn't* that yucky corn be yummy *this* time? Crazy makes sense in a crazy world.

Sense, alas, does not. I know I'm going to catch a lot of flak from the earnest early childhood googoos who believe children should be respected at all times and that you should reason with them. But . . . *bwah-ha-ha-ha!*

Seriously? Have you ever *tried* reasoning with a four-year-old? It's hard enough reasoning with an *adult* who wants something. And if you think I'm exaggerating, then explain to me the ridiculous amount of credit card debt in this country.

But if you absolutely need to be convinced, go ahead and try reasoning with a child. I dare you. Start by offering a reasonable instruction and wait for the inevitable "Why?" Next, explain patiently and rationally.

How did that go? Disastrously? Okay, that's normal. Now, here is where Einstein's quasi-theory of insanity sets

wrong

"Quit making a mess and get up to bed!"

right

"Hey, who wants to stay up and help me clean?"

up an interesting tension. What are you supposed to do the *next* time you confront that four-year-old? *Reason* with him?

Since that's what failed the first time, the Einstein principle tells you that sanity would be insane. Ha! A paradox worthy of . . . well, of Einstein.

So if you can't reason with a four-year-old, what do you do?

You *un*-reason with him. That's what you do.

In other words, talk crazy talk. But crazy talk that makes perfect sense within the construct of whatever insanity they are going through. Like, when asked, "Can we have cookies for breakfast?"

You can answer, "*Can* we? Why, we practically *have* to! Didn't you know? Today is National Monkey Day, and the traditional meal for National Monkey Day is Cookies for Breakfast. But not just any cookies. Monkey cookies. Which is the official monkey name for sliced bananas. Yaaay! Cookies for breakfast!"

Not that un-reasoning is guaranteed or even intended to succeed. It is only to establish enough un-reasonable credibility with the child before paralyzing his mental circuits.

But the insanity is not all bad. The very same madness that makes a four-year-old maddening can also make her charming, which explains the staying power of "The Family Circus." And four seems to be the magic age for charming nonsense talk. It is just past the Terrible Threes, which every insider knows are worse than the Terrible Twos but don't have the same reputation because Therrible Threes is less tripping on the tongue. And it is just prior to the prekindergarten anxiety that can be such a trying time for child and parent.

Mainly, though, it is a time when a proficiency in speech overlaps most with a deficiency in logic. The result is that your child becomes a veritable funny-saying machine.

My older daughter had us—and every other grown-up in earshot—in stitches most of the time. I wished I could have captured one one-hundredth of it on tape or on paper. But I was usually too busy with her one-year-old sister to grab a pen or recorder and was too brain damaged to remember later. Here are just a few gems:

"If I ate some animal crackers, I'd have all kinds of crazy poops!"

"Come onnnn. Can't we just talk about candy and whatever we want?"

And the deliciously inexplicable, "Welcome . . . to *Cheese Victory!*"

Often it wasn't the words that were so funny but the delivery. Had I the presence of mind to put a wire on her for that year, I could have sold MP3s of her quotes on iTunes and paid for her college education.

As I write, her younger sister is entering that crazy-talk sweet spot. Will she follow in her sister's footsteps? It's still too soon to tell. If so, I hope to capture more of it this time around. A few days back, I did overhear this promising pretend phone call from the backseat as we were on our errand adventures. For full effect, try to hear it in a toddler's pretend-voice falsetto.

(Boop boop.)

Hello, birds?

Hello.

Do you eat worms and bugs and seeds and sometimes ants?

Yes, we do.

Okay. Bye.

I called a bird on a raisin.

Can you believe it? She was placing a call on a raisin—on the north side of Chicago where cell phone reception is atrocious. See what I mean? Crazy!

The Parent's Serenity Prayer

God, grant me the grace to accept the things that cannot be cleaned,

the courage to clean the things I can,

and the wisdom to know the difference.

"Laundry or composting?"

CHAPTER 23

More Ask Captain Dad!

The truth can hurt. That's why I make up most of what I tell my kids.

Yes, it's time for another misinformative installment of "Ask Captain Dad." Let's start with a question my daughters posed one day during a rainy spring.

"Why are they called toadstools? Are they stools for toads?"

Captain Dad: No. They are not stools for toads, because toads are too big and would crush them. Toadstools, you see, are not toad stools, but toad's *tools.* As in tools for a toad. There is a species of toad native to the Seychelles Islands (where the world's

greatest seashells can be found; hence the name) that has been known to pluck three or four toadstools and turn them over to reveal the flat of the button head. Then they overlay them with twigs and reeds to create an elevated flat surface upon which they then sit, sort of like a . . . Oh, I don't know what you'd call it. Sort of a small chair without a back.

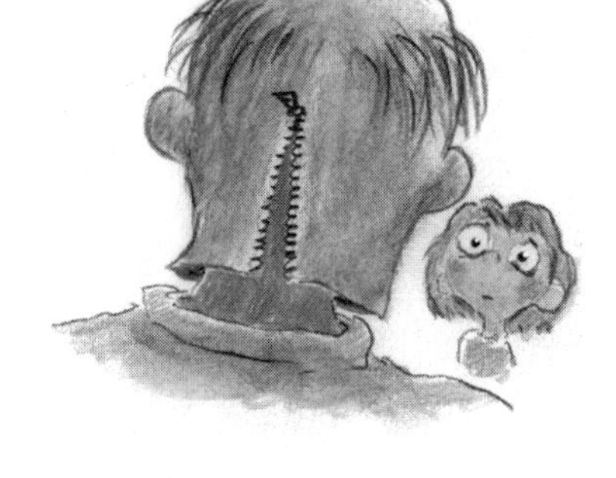

"Are you and Mom really just space aliens in disguise?"

Captain Dad: Of course not! Now drink your Windex or you won't get any moldy sponges for dessert.

Whys Beyond My Years: Some "Why" Questions to Which There Is No Acceptable Answer

- Why did you give me *this* cup?
- Why did my *sister* get the pink bowl?
- Why do you think it's annoying when I speak in dolphin?

CHAPTER 24

The Preschool Death March

At this point in the book it's too late to save my reputation, so I may as well confess.

My wife and I waited until *after* our first child was born to start looking for schools. There. I said it. Nothing can redeem us from such egregious neglect. But since I've got some time to kill before DCFS comes to haul the kids away, I may as well tell you the story of the pathetic little we did to place our child in the Best Schools.

We started when our daughter was two. And a half. (Oh, my God! These people are monsters!) We started with the usual online searching and asking around. Asking around was interesting. It was like shopping for a religion. Nearly every preschool people sent their children to was described as "the best."

"Oh, we *loved* it there," they'd coo. To be fair, this is the response I technically wanted to hear. Except . . .

Well, the *words* were what I wanted to hear, but the pop-eyed reverence in their voices kind of creeped me out. I don't know, is that just a guy thing? I mean, if someone just said with a nod, "Yeah, it's good. Our [insert child's name here] really liked it. She got to do dress up a lot," *that* would have gotten me. But their proselytizing "We *loved* it" made me leery.

Neighbors started dropping off flyers in our mailbox for their favorite preschools. People on the playground, folks in my wife's

LI'L HARVARD
A+
ABCs OF LIFE
BABY TESLA PRE-SCHOOL

office, everybody had a recommendation. Love stories, horror stories, fear mongering, reassurance. All the tips you could ever ask for. Even my wife's hairdresser was lobbying for her kids' pre–alma mater.

Where our daughter did her dress up and finger painting would apparently dictate where she went to college.

So we dutifully drew up a list of every preschool within a five-mile radius. It helped that Lake Michigan, less than three miles to the east of us, knocked a chunk off our search area.

Our first effort to thin the herd was to eliminate schools that were not accredited. That instantly brought us down to a manageable scrum. Then we struck various Best Schools from our list for reasons unrelated to their relative Best-ness. Such as the French School. As attractive as it was to think that our gifted prescholar would learn to color in French, we concluded that she would have to color like Monet to justify the fourteen-thousand-dollars-a-year *preschool* tuition.

There were several other preschool contestants that charged even higher tuition. We calculated that our child's education would easily top a million dollars if we didn't consider more humble beginnings. Given that we were expecting our second million-dollar baby at the time, humble seemed a better choice than bankrupt.

We continued to consider multilingual schools though. (Even the British School, which sort of counts. At least for Americans.) One drawback of having a stay-at-home parent instead of a nanny or au pair is that you don't typically learn another language

"He goes to a real party preschool."

that isn't already spoken at home. In our house, it's only English and Gibberish.

Little by little we chipped away. We called one school for a brochure, only to be met with a snippy, "All that information is online." Boom. Off the list. Some schools didn't admit kids under four, thus setting them at a marked disadvantage in the all-important Macaroni Art section of the SAT. Boom. Off the list.

One school sent us their brochure and application forms. But after that, they were impossible to reach, refusing to return our calls and e-mails. I suppose they were only living up to their reputation of being exclusive.

Eventually we got down to an Elite Eight. Over the next couple of months, we would fill out forms, craft various three-word descriptions of our child, attend open houses, and schedule interviews and class visits with and without our daughter. And we would sit in some of the smallest chairs imaginable with other smiling couples, all of them looking similarly overwhelmed.

The parents we encountered were a rather diverse group of upper-middle-class white people. Among them were the type who shamelessly schmoozed the principals, asking probing questions about the school's mission statement and the high schools and colleges their preschoolers typically matriculate into. Others, meanwhile, looked stunned, as if they thought they had left their competitive school-sports days behind in their ninth-grade gym locker. Then, of course, there were the class clowns sitting off to the side, snickering to themselves. Okay, *our*selves.

This was particularly the case during the mandatory three-hour open house at a school that kept calling the word *cultish* to my mind. I couldn't say *cultish* out loud for a variety of reasons, not the least of which was that it was where my wife had gone to preschool when she was three. She *loved* it. She only seemed to

> I dropped my younger daughter off at her very first day of preschool with a kiss and said, "Have a good first day at school, my big girl."
>
> Her reply? "Okay. Your kisses are germy." Ah, tender memories.

have one memory of the place, but it was a very fond memory. They had made fresh-squeezed orange juice in the classroom one day. "I would *never* have been able to do that at home," she gushed. Of course not. She wouldn't have been allowed in the house with a wet bathing suit for the same reason. Her mother was sane.

But cultish or not, even I had to concede that the OJ squeezing was pretty cool. And schools of this persuasion are known for producing children who always, always, always put away their toys. Heck, I'd even send my kids to a head-shaving, pamphlet-peddling cult if it could drill that into them. So off we went to the mandatory three-hour open house/indoctrination/reeducation with bagels and coffee. Everyone wore name tags, the only purpose of which seemed to be to estimate people's ages by noting who was a John or a Jane and who was a Justin or a Heather. Because, Lord knows, we were all too intimidated to socialize. The presentation room, you see, was also the student lounge. It was veritably wallpapered with precocious literary quotes and posters for films that people seldom talk about except to the smell of clove cigarettes.

The first hour kicked off with a propaganda film extolling the Innovative Educational Philosophy, created by their esteemed Founder, and praising the kids educated under this paradigm and even crediting some of them for working on the film.

Once primed, hour two treated us to a tour of the premises. We were broken into smaller groups and assigned a guide who ushered us through the halls, stopping to talk to groups of

Some Questions You Might Not Think to Ask (but Later Will Wish You Did)

- Is there a sandbox students will get to wallow in each day at recess?
- Will we be charged for replacing all the sand that comes home in their shoes?
- Is paper encouraged, or is painting directly to clothing the preferred medium?
- Do your teachers have any tattoos or body piercings that will result in an awkward conversation between me and my impressionable young child?
- Do you serve students anything other than high-concentrate liquid sugar (a.k.a. juice) at snack time?
- Can I write one single check up front instead of getting constantly nickeled-and-dimed for fundraisers, field trips, and random special events?

youngsters working on presumably precocious projects here and there (that is, the guide talked to them; we lowly parents were severely instructed *not* to talk to students). On the stairs she paused to genuflect before a large oil portrait of the Founder. The Founder, she trilled, sought to promote each child's individuality and personal genius, to free them to express themselves and . . .

That's when it struck me that throughout all these many hallways I did not see a single scrap of student art in a display case, on a classroom wall or window, or even taped to a locker. I bit my tongue, and we trundled along to our first classroom audit.

It was a spectacular classroom, without question. Huge, open, full of light. All the parents were rightfully in awe. My wife and I took our usual place, on the fringe. As the tour guide's lecture began, we found ourselves standing next to the Live Thing habitat. We had been informed in the first hour that it was in the school's Philosophy to keep Live Things in the classroom. Not just plants, but animals, too.

To my eye, however, something was amiss. I didn't want to mention anything, lest I exacerbate my image as a heckler. But my wife noticed it, too. She gave me a meaningful look and nodded toward an unusually lethargic hamster.

"I know," I whispered. "I thought so, too. But it can't be, really, can it?"

As if on cue, a seven-year-old boy stepped up and said, "Our hamster died." Just like that. Matter-of-fact. He might just as well have said, "We had cupcakes for snack yesterday," for all the import he gave it.

Indeed the hamster in the cage was dead. It had ceased to be. Expired and gone to meet its maker. An ex-hamster.

But there he lay, not haphazardly as if it had just happened with the prospective school parents massing in the hall, leaving no one a moment to flush him down the toilet yet. He was on display, lying in state.

The tour moved on, but my wife could not let the incident go. Me, I said nothing. We weren't halfway through with the morning's program, and it was already looking up for me. Hope was alive that we would be able to cross this one off the list without me ever having to slur her pre–alma mater with telepathic insinuations of the word *cultish*.

In truth, I didn't want to slur it at all. It did have an Innovative Educational Philosophy that was genuinely innovative. And

I like to think of myself as being generally in favor of innovation. But innovation, as I had been taught in school, did not normally include jettisoning all the useful artifacts of the thing being improved upon.

For instance, when innovators added ball bearings to the wheel, they did not get rid of all the bits that identified it as a wheel. Like the roundness or the axle. So it puzzled me why an innovative school would get rid of the very things that make schools schools. Like tests. I mean, wouldn't tests prove the Innovative Educational Philosophy's superiority?

> "I want a pet when I grow up, but not a dust bunny because those make me cough."
>
> Lucy, age 4

I was heartened to hear my wife probe this issue during the third hour's panel interview of student prodigies.

"Is it true," she asked? "Really? Are you honestly telling me that, even knowing how high schools rely on admissions tests, you never, ever, even once, had a test?"

One seventh-grader broke under questioning. No, it was *not* true, he confessed. "We had a science test once."

A. Science test. Once.

The words barely had a chance to register before another of the school's academic A-Team chimed in, "But it didn't count for anything."

Dead hamster. One measly test that counted for nothing. And nobody mentioned that they still let them make orange

"Four 'Greats,' one 'Super-Duper,' and a 'Special.' What's with the 'Special?'"

juice. Somehow we would have to live without a kid who picks up her toys. As the casting directors say, "Next!"

Aside from the rodent-in-state episode, the three-hour tour and the nonexistent testing, the rest of the experience was surprisingly typical of our other preschool adventures. The bagels, the room visits, the Q&As. And, of course, the name tags.

We had looked at a variety of schools, too. Not just private ones with fancy Philosophies. We checked out public schools. Okay, we were *obliged* to look at public schools, given my wife's position on the public payroll.

So we visited one that had a writing-based curriculum. It looked like a natural fit for our daughter who was in love with letters. Until we learned that she would have to forsake *x* and *y*. Too math-y, which was not strictly a part of the curriculum.

Another school eighty-sixed.

The Catholic schools offered lots of great choices, and we were obligated to check them out, too. I enjoyed sixteen years of Catholic education, and my brother is a man of the cloth. My wife acquired her bachelor and law degrees from Jesuit universities. She even taught in a Catholic high school her first year out of college.

But the Catholic schools all started at the ungodly early hour of eight o'clock. Getting a three-and-a-half-year-old out of the house at that hour with a six-month-old underfoot as well? What did God want of us?

Ultimately we compromised on our public-parochial obligations and sent our daughter to a Lutheran school. It was right on my wife's way to work. And it started at nine o'clock.

So, how did that work out? It was good. Our Rebecca really liked it. She got to do dress up a lot.

CHAPTER 25

Adventures in Toilet Training

Over the last year or two, people have been asking me if I've lost weight. I'd be more pleased if they asked if I were getting taller or if my hair were getting thicker, but I take what I can get.

Anyway, I haven't lost any weight. Not really. But I *do* look noticeably slimmer.

I'm not packing a spare diaper in my pocket anymore. Sweet freedom!

Except not entirely. Now I always have to be on the lookout for the nearest toilet. I plan my every step accordingly, like a polar bear leaping from ice floe to ice floe, always thinking one floe ahead.

Kids, you see, aren't exactly planners. When they have to go, they have to go *now.* You can ask them to hold it, but you just might be in the middle of a traffic jam. On the expressway. With road construction and detours and nowhere to pull over even if there were a public restroom you could reach. Or even a bush. So you implore that big kid—emphasizing the words *big kid*—to be strong until you can reach the first available gas station or fast-food joint with a semi-legal parking space. Only five minutes. Pleeeeeeeeeeeeeeeeeze.

Have you ever wondered why kids need booster seats in the car until they are eight? (No, I am absolutely not changing the subject.) When you finally pull into the Popeye's parking lot and scramble around to the backseat door to whisk your "big kid" inside to the restroom, you can tell by the sheepish look that she couldn't hold all of it in (but most, thank God). With somewhat less urgency you go inside and buy a drink to pay the restroom tax while your big kid, grateful to be wearing dark colors, slinks into the ladies' room to finish the job. You shrug it off outwardly, but secretly worry if the car will stink—and just when you thought you were finally going to get around to trading it in to buy that newer car.

But—lo and behold!—the booster seat upholstery has soaked it all up. And it's machine washable!

And *that's* why kids need booster seats until they are at least eight. To protect your car from having urine-soaked upholstery. You won't always be so lucky, but you learn to count even the small victories.

Small, that is, compared to that first major triumph of getting your baby to simply sit on the potty for the first time. You will have tried positive reinforcement, the promise of "big girl underpants," desperate pleading, and outright bribery before she finally decides she's going to do it on her own. Which is why toilet-training experts advocate waiting until the child is ready to use the toilet on her own. The problem is, as wonderful as modern disposable diapers are, they can be *too* wonderful when a kid doesn't want to give them up. Think about it: Imagine having your own portable toilet that doesn't require you to leave your seat to take care of business—with no subsequent discomfort. And someone else will clean up the mess. Sounds pretty sweet, huh? So you can hardly blame kids these days.

Still, like a kid who has to go, sometimes *you* can't wait. The condition for being able to start most preschools is that kids need to be able to use the toilet. On their own.

So, on an Independence Day not too many Independence Days ago, we found ourselves with a toddler who seemed utterly content to outsource the disposal of her bodily waste. With preschool scheduled to start in less than two months, my wife and I were white-knuckled and desperate. Me especially. My daughter's starting preschool meant *my* independence. For a couple hours a day, at least.

My wife was ready to bribe her with candy from the get-go. Me, I insisted on winning this battle on principle. "You can do this! You're a big girl. I know you can."

Finally, one day my little three-year-old walked into the bathroom—on her own, without telling anybody—sat down, and piddled into the plastic potty. As soon as we realized what was going on, we cheered, we gushed, she beamed with pride. I thought I had won.

Until she demanded her candy.

I stammered. My wife smiled. It was already there in the bathroom waiting for her.

Anyway, we were off and running. Well, sometimes running. Sometimes merely walking fast—as fast as possible with knees pressed together.

Now this is where dads with daughters can have it rougher than moms with sons. Outside the home, moms can take kids into any restroom they want and no one will blink. We dads have a quandary: In the men's room, I may have to explain those funny sinks on the wall and other funny stuff. I shudder at the thought of ever overhearing my daughter having a tea party pretending to serve her dollies "urinal cakes." And let's be honest, a lot of men's rooms have all the sanitariness of a swamp.

Yet the other alternative can be even more daunting. On more than one occasion when my gender didn't happen to match the one on the door, I have been brusquely informed, "This is the *Ladies'* room."

"And *this* is the lady," I huffed back.

Go ahead, make me suffer the changing-table inequity. I'm man enough to take it. But don't keep me from treating my little lady like a lady, especially when her bladder is distended like a weather balloon. And double especially when all the ladies' rooms I'm talking about are ones with only one commode; so it's not like anyone else is going to be in there.

Even if someone else *is* going to be in there, didn't you read the part about my loss of testosterone from being around kids all day? Add to that my being surrounded by females, and my estrogen levels are probably high enough to qualify me for the women's competition in the Olympics. Not that you'd know it from the way my hair is receding.

And one of the reasons it is receding, I'd venture, is because of all this restroom-related stress.

So maybe I should answer that question about my slimming down differently: Yes, I *have* lost weight. But it's all hair weight.

Developmental Milestones—Not Theirs, Yours!

- No longer having to keep track of months—or weeks—and simply being able to say, "She's two" for a whole year.

- Taking down the gates that help prevent your infant or toddler from falling down the stairs, but cause you to trip and practically break your neck at least twice a day.

- Throwing away the baby bottles and nipples, and giving away the breast pump.

"I'm all for pushing them out of the nest, but maybe next time we could wait till they hatch."

- Switching from formula to cow's milk and not having to smell formula—or the weird poop smell that comes with it—ever again.

- Using the toilet with the door closed the whole time and no one asking you, "Can I see it?" before you flush.

Epilogue

If I Knew Then . . .

As the pages grow thin, I can hear you wondering, "If you knew then what you know now, what would you do differently?" Or maybe that's only a sleep deprivation–induced hallucination I'm hearing. But it's a good question nevertheless. And I do have a few more pages to fill, so let me take a crack at it. Here goes.

Ahem.

I actually knew more as a new parent than I know now. I had read all the books. I had digested stacks of manuals on everything from indigestion to breast milk storage, even though my breasts were not the ones making the milk. I learned how to identify and treat various rashes. I studied modern discipline techniques and memorized all the cognitive-development milestones. If there was a "New Parent" Jeopardy, I'd have been grand champion.

"Cradle Cap for 500, Alex."

But that was then. Today nearly everything I knew is gone due to the aforementioned sleep deprivation and intellectual discourse on the level of, "You're boots."

"No, I'm shoes. *You're* boots!" (Note to self: When my little one gets older, remind me to ask her what "You're boots" meant.)

In short, my brain has turned to mush. And it has made me a better parent.

If I had known that when I started out, I would have relaxed more. I would have trusted the books less. I should have known to do that anyway, what with how much the books contradict each other. But see "sleep deprivation," above. Books also don't give you the most salient details. For instance, when the sleep gurus tell you to let your child "cry it out" in the middle of the night, they don't mean when the baby is only fifteen months old. So you really *should* go into your baby's room and check, instead of waiting until morning to discover that she has spray-painted her crib and everything in it with two quarts of vomit. I wish I had known that. Ohhh, how I wish I had known that.

I'm glad I *didn't* know how physically painful it would be. Don't let the short pants fool you; I'm not as young as I look. Everything at my age is *supposed* to hurt already, but throw in bad feet and chasing two little girls who are the kind that older ladies call "very busy," and ow. Ow, ow, ow. If I had known that, pain aversion might have put me off kids altogether.

But this is only more proof that, when embarking on life's biggest challenges, it's best to go in deluded. The only way I believe anyone can be an effective parent is by *not* knowing that they *can't*.

Which happens to be the one thing that the books are actually good at telling you. Not how to be an effective parent, but that YOU CAN'T DO IT. Under the guise of being helpful, they are written to make you feel inadequate. If I ever write a how-to book on parenting, it will be titled, *You're Doing It Wrong*. And here's what it would say inside: "You're doing it wrong." That's it. The rest would be glowing blurbs of endorsement from every parenting authority on the planet. Well, maybe not *every* parenting authority. There wouldn't be enough room. But maybe that's good: That gives me a sequel.

Random strangers also consider themselves authorities. They can't stop themselves. I would like to portray stay-at-home dads as the worst victims of advice abuse, on the premise that everyone assumes we are clueless boobs simply because we are boobless. But I understand that stay-at-home moms also get both ears full of unsolicited advice. So I lodge this plea on all of our behalf.

Please, everybody, show a little professional courtesy to working parents. By which I mean people whose work is parenting. Stow the advice.

Take the time I was walking my five-month-old daughter in a stroller. About twenty-five minutes into our stroll, she emitted a hiccup.

One. Single. Freaking. Hiccup.

Of course this was precisely the moment we passed our first fellow pedestrian in about ten of those minutes. It was a "helpful" older woman who instantly observed that my daughter was getting too much dairy. I told her that she was still being breastfed. Not only that, but she had hiccuped in the womb.

Aha! The woman countered that it was my *wife* who was eating too much dairy. (It is true that my wife *probably* had a nibble of cheese *somewhere* during the nine months of her pregnancy, but I wouldn't swear to that.) Had I still known everything I had read five months earlier, before the sleepless nights, I would have called the woman an idiot, berated her for presuming to know more about parenting—not to mention my daughter and wife—than I did, and issued her a sound thrashing. Resulting in my incarceration.

But!

Thanks to the mush-brain effect, I was able to smile wanly and walk away, to live to parent another day.

So this is my point. Hiccups happen in parenting. Who knows why? Who cares? You don't *have* to know everything. All

you do have to know is that you have to keep doing it—even when everybody says you're doing it wrong.

And everybody does apparently say that in the widely publicized Mommy Wars, which allegedly pit the Stay-at-Home Moms against the Working Moms in an ideological cage match, not that I can imagine many Real Moms of either stripe having much time left over for ideology after they put the kids to bed.

There are Daddy Wars, too, but it's a very different situation. There aren't enough of us stay-at-home guys—yet—to make this a real fight. For now, in fact, it is more aptly called the War on Dads. It's that one-sided.

It is so one-sided that it is literally a joke. A whole sitcom. In fact, *every* sitcom. Yes, since Al Bundy (the anti–Dr. Huxtable), the entire institution of pop culture has sold dads down the river and tossed gas on the flames of the feeding frenzy. And if you think *that* is an embarrassing stew of clichés, just flick on the tube for another episode of *Father Knows Squat.*

The average TV dad these days has about as much general competence as Shemp.[7] Any dad who even tries to be competent with children has to atone for it with insecurities about becoming overly feminized *(Parenthood)* or by being overly feminized to begin with *(Modern Family)*.

Why?

Are non–Homer Simpson dads somehow offensive to us? Are they intimidating to women? Other men? To single young nitwits who were raised by TV and can only regurgitate fictional stereotypes in the scripts they write? What? Who?

How? How do they come up with such lunacy?

But they do, and they're not alone. The image of the goofus-aloofus dad has permeated our culture.

When I started writing about being a Captain Dad, I was advised to portray myself as a boob, a bungler, a stumblebum. Otherwise, I was sternly lectured, no woman would ever read what I wrote.

Seriously?

....

7 Note to my female readers: Shemp was the original third Stooge, before Curly. I'm sorry, I didn't mean to exclude you from my remarks as much as I meant to score a direct hit with the male readers, who have a genetically encoded knowledge of, and affinity for, all things Stooges. You can look it up; it's on the y-I-oughta chromosome.

"We're going to the park to size up the competition."

Call me crazy (yet again), but I kind of imagine that a woman would *want* a man to be competent, responsible, and trustworthy with kids. Especially her own. Whether he stays home with them all day or not. The ideal man, after all, is the guy who can do anything, is he not? Well, isn't taking care of the kids something?

Take the dad I saw with his daughter in the food court last Friday. He didn't strike me as the type you'd cast as a stay-at-home, but he kept pace with his girl, step for step, as she ran on about the off-brand fairies in her coloring book. He didn't even break a sweat. He couldn't have been more comfortable if he were talking about industrial fasteners or the likelihood of the White Sox pitching a perfect game.

In other words, he was a guy. A *real* guy. Better than that. A dad. Not just a guy playing one on TV.

So lay off dads, popular culture. Like the old song says,

I can bring home the bacon,

Fry it up in a pan,

And never let you forget I can't eat it because of my

cholesterol, man.

And let's not forget that more and more studies are coming out about the advantages of growing up in a solid family with a father, especially a caring one. I'd think that, in this era of parenting as a contact sport, this competitive edge alone would justify encouraging men to be more, well, manly. Fatherly.

If I became a stay-at-home dad for any ideological reason, it was just as that great modern philosopher says: "Git 'r done."

Someone had to do it. Period.

As long as my wife is already serving our children through public service, that someone will be me. When the kids are finally in school all day, then I can get to repairing the ten-year hole in my résumé.

In the end, raising children is not a woman's job or a man's job. It's all of our job. The country *needs* children, after all, if only to pay our Social Security when we get older. And I am proud to say that, like my mother, I have not shirked my duty in the World's Toughest Job.

And as for my children? Yes, of course, I love them beyond measure. Every silly, cute, crazy, maddening, infuriating, adorable molecule of them. Even if I am desperately looking forward to a few minutes to myself.

> "Sometimes I dance all day just listening to my heart."
>
> Rebecca, age 4

One day they will be off to college, then on to lives of their own. People say I'm going to miss this time while they were young, and I'm sure they're right. But I know I won't miss it as much as a lot of other, less-fortunate dads. Because I *didn't* miss it.

Not one silly, cute, crazy, maddening, infuriating, adorable minute of it.

Book Club Questions

1. How did you and your spouse decide who would stay home with the kids, assuming that was an option?

2. You obviously have kids. How did you find the time to read a book, let alone join a book club?

3. Who's watching your kids while you're out throwing back a glass of Merlot with your "book club," hmm?

4. What is your child's Superfriend? How do you keep track of it, especially at bedtime?

5. Tell about a time you lost your child. How did you find him or her? How long was it before you admitted it to anyone?

6. What invention would you wish for to make parenting easier?

7. Why do you give your child juice when all the doctors and dentists say not to?

8. If your child could have one superpower, what would you want it to be?

9. Please tell us how you've gotten your kids to put away their toys. Or if.

10. While we're at it, any ideas on getting them to eat their vegetables? Brush their hair without complaining/screaming/crying? Remember to close the refrigerator door? . . .

"I swore I wouldn't make the same mistakes with my children as my parents did."

Acknowledgments

The kids are turning out well enough that the author feels it is safe to acknowledge his parents, Pat and Marie Byrnes, for their sterling example; following it seems to be working. He is further grateful to his agent, Amy Rennert, and editor, Lara Asher, for their enthusiastic support. As for the Hungerdungers, the men in his so-called writers group, he promises to thank them for their moral support in proper writerly fashion, with beer. Lastly, he wishes to thank his utterly amazing wife, Lisa, not only for her patience and encouragement, but also for her fearless editing and flawless instincts.

About the Author

Best known as a cartoonist for the *New Yorker*, author of the cartoon anthology *What Would Satan Do?*, and regular contributor to WhatToExpect.com's "Word of Mom," Pat Byrnes started his career as an aerospace engineer. Thinking advertising would be a quicker path to cartooning, he became a copywriter, then a voiceover actor, then an illustrator, all the while moonlighting in improv and other, more adventurous comedy acts on stage and radio. Not so quick a path, after all. But he later drew on all of that experience to invent the iPhone and Web app Smurks, which serves both as an emotional rating system for public feedback as well as a breakthrough tool in emotional health, most strikingly for people with autistic spectrum disorder. His previous stay-at-home parenting experience was only in cartoon form, in his syndicated comic strip "Monkeyhouse," about a philosophical nine-year-old girl and her widowed dad. In 2003 he married Illinois Attorney General Lisa Madigan, better known in his world as "Mommy." They live with their radiant daughters on the banks of the Chicago River. You can follow his continuing adventures in stay-at-home parenting at CaptainDad.com.